D1263074

THE NEGRO MOTORIST GREEN-BOOK

1940 FACSIMILE EDITION

VICTOR H. GREEN

Published by Victor H. Green

www.snowballpublishing.com

info@snowballpublishing.com

For information regarding special discounts for bulk purchases, please contact Snowball Publishing at

sale@snowballpublishing.com

THE

NEGRO MOTORIST

GREEN BOOK

ESTABLISHED 1936

WILLIAM H. GREEN
EDITOR

JOHN C. DILLARD
CIRCULATION MGR.

INTRODUCTION

The idea of "The Green Book" is to give the Motorist and Tourist a Guide not only of the Hotels and Tourist Homes in all of the large cities, but other classifications that will be found useful wherever he may be. Also facts and information that the Negro Motorist can use and depend upon.

There are thousands of places that the public doesn't know about and aren't listed. Perhaps you might know of some? If so send in their names and addresses and the kind of business, so that we might pass it along to the rest of your fellow Motorists.

You will find it handy on your travels, whether at home or in some other state, and is up to date. Each year we are compiling new lists as some of these places move, or go out of business and new business places are started giving added employment to members of our race.

When you are traveling mention "The Green Book" so as to let these people know just how you found out about their place of business. If they haven't heard about This Guide, tell them to get in touch with us.

If this Guide is useful, let us know, if not tell us also, as we appreciate your criticisms.

If any errors are found, kindly notify the publishers so that they can be corrected in the next issue.

Published yearly in the month of April by Victor H. Green. Executive & Advertising office at 938 St. Nicholas Ave., New York, N. Y. William H. Green, Editor; John C. Dillard, Circulation Manager. Advertising Office at 938 St. Nicholas Ave., Telephone ED. 4-3425.

 Manuscripts submitted for publication should be sent to 938 St. Nicholas Ave. New York, N. Y., and must be accompanied by return postage. No liability can be assumed for the loss or damage to manuscripts although every possible precaution will be taken.

Subscription: Twenty-five cents per copy.

Advertising: For rates, Write to the publisher.

Last forms close on March 15th. We reserve the right to reject any advertising which in our opinion that does not conform to our standards.

Correspondence to the Publisher

327 Railroad Ave.,
Hackensack, N. J.

Victor H. Green
Publisher
938 St. Nicholas Ave.
New York, N. Y.

Dear Sir;

It is a great pleasure for me to give credit where credit is due. Many of my friends have joined me in admitting that "The Negro Motorist Green Book" is a credit to the Negro Race. It is a book badly needed among our Race since the advance of the motor age. Realizing the only way we knew where and how to reach our pleasure resorts was in a way of speaking, by word of mouth, until the publication of "The Negro Motorist Green Book." With our wishes of your success, and your earnest efforts. We earnestly believe "The Negro Motorist Green Book" will mean as much if not more to us as the A. A. A. means to the white race.

Respectfully Yours,

Wm. Smith.

INDEX

CARD OF APPRECIATION

The Publishers of this guide wish to publically thank the following people and newspapers who have contributed and worked to bring this Travel Guide before the public and up to date, so that we as a race might have something authenic to travel by and to make traveling better for the Negro.

Mr. James (Billboard) Jackson—Special Rept. of the Standard Oil.
Mr. Chas. A. R. McDowell—of The United States Travel Bureau.
Mr. John D. Long—of New York City, N. Y.
Mr. Elmer Jackson—of Kansas City, Mo.
Mrs. Ella Glenn—of Springfied, Ohio.
The Louisville Leader—of Louisville Ky.
The Cleveland Call & Post—of Cleveland, Ohio.

We hope that you in reading this will tell others about this guide so that they will know of its usefullness.

We have given you a selection of listings at you might chose from, under no circumstances do these listings imply that the place is recommended.

EXPLANATION

We are making this guide as near complete as possible until such time as we can get the information from the different sections of the country.

The business classifications listed have been arranged under the different cities and towns, so that one won't have any trouble finding what they want.

ALABAMA

ANDALUSIA

HOTELS
New Dunbar—323 N. 17th St.

TOURIST HOMES
Mrs. Ed. Andrews—
69 N. Cotton St.

BIRMINGHAM

HOTELS
Dunbar Hotel—316 N. 17th St.
Fraternal Hotel—1619 N. 4th St.
Palm Leaf Hotel—318 N. 18th St.
Rush Hotel—316 N. 18th St.

TAVERNS
Peoples Cafe—317 N. 17 St.

DECATUR

TOURIST HOMES
Mrs. F. Hayes—207 W. Church St.

GADSDEN

HOTELS
Smith Hotel—902 Garden Ave.

TOURIST HOMES
Mrs. S. Neal—1317 4th Aev.
Mrs. A. Sheperd—1324 4th Ave.
Mrs. J. Simons—233 N. 6 St.

GENEVA

TOURIST HOMES
Joe Dondal
Susie M. Sharp
Sallie Edwards

MOBILE

TOURIST HOMES
Mrs. E. Reed—950 Lyons St.
Mrs. E. Jordan—256 N. Dearborn
Mrs. G. B. Sylvester—355 Cuba St.
Mrs. F. Wildins 254 N. Dearbon St.

BEAUTY PARLORS
Ritz—607 Congress St.

SHEFFIELD

HOTELS
McClain Hotel—19th St.

TOURIST HOMES
Mrs. I. Hawkins—S. Atlantic Ave.

TROY

TOURIST HOMES
Mrs. S. A. Benton—
113 E. FairView St.
Mrs. J. Thomas—E. Academy St.

TUSCALOOSO

TOURIST HOMES
Mrs. G. W. Baugh—2526 12th St.
Mrs. M. A. Barnes—419 30th Ave.
Mrs. G. W. Clopton—1516 25th Ave.
Mrs. G. Robinson—11th St.

ARIZONA

NOGALES

RESTAURANTS
BELL'S CAFE
325 MORLEY AVE.

PHOENIX

HOTELS
Raymond—607 E. Jefferson St.
St. Louis—535 E. Jefferson St.
Rice's—535 E. Jefferson
St. Louis Hotel
Thomas E. Lewis Hotel

TOURIST HOMES
Gardner's—1229 E. Wash. St.

GARAGES
Tourist—122—S. First St.

RESTAURANTS
J. Mayse Lunch Room 46-2nd St.
Alhambia—246 E. Wash. St.
Tapps—39 So. 2nd St.

SERVICE STATIONS
Shell—1030 E. Washington St.
Stewarts—11th St. & Wash.

BEAUTY PARLORS
Copelands—1316 E. Jefferson St.

BARBER SHOPS
Hagler's—106 So. 2nd St.

NIGHT CLUBS
Elks—7th Ave. & Tonto

TUCSON

TOURIST HOMES
Mrs. G. W. Obie—738 No. 10th Ave.

RESTAURANT
Rainbow Grill—91 W. Jackson

SERVICE STATIONS
Washington—Cor. Main &
St. Marye

ARKANSAS

ARKADELPHIA

HOTELS
HILL HOTEL
16 PINE ST.
Trigg's—Caddo St.

TOURIST HOMES
Mrs. B. Dedman—W. Caddo St.
Mrs. L. Cooper—W. Pine St.
P. Anderson—W. Caddo St.
Millers—3rd & Alabama Sts.

RESTAURANTS
Richie Square Deal—Caddo St.
Hill's—River St.
Turner's—Caddo St.

BARBER SHOPS
Scott's—6th & Clay St.
Richie's Upright—16th St.

EL DORADO

HOTELS
Brewster—E. & B. Sts.
Green—S. Hill St.

TOURIST HOMES
C. W. Moore—5th & Lincoln Ave.
Dr. Dunning—7th & Columbia Ave.

FAYETTEVILLE

HOTELS
Mebbs—9 N. Willow St.

TOURIST HOMES
Mrs. S. Manuel—313 Olive St.
Mrs. N. Smith—259 E. Center St.

FORT SMITH

HOTELS
The Stratford—1208 - 9th St.
Ullery Inn—719 N. 9th St.

TOURIST HOMES
E. O. Trent—1301 N. 9th St.

HELENA

TOURIST HOMES
Mrs. G. W. Prosser—306 Beech St.
Mrs. B. W. Crump—103 Briscoe St.

HOT SPRINGS

HOTELS
The Claridy House—410 Cottage St.
Crittenden—314 Cottage St.
The Reed House—115 Cottage St.
Woodman—511 Malvern

TOURIST HOMES
Mrs. J. H. Barabin—
717 Peasant St.
Mrs. J. W. Rife—
347½ Malvern Ave.
Mrs. N. Fletcher—416 Pleasant St.
Mrs. H. Greyer—234 Garden St.
Mrs. C. C. Wison—232 Garden St.
Mrs. H. Stilson—
735 Pleasant St.
Mrs. E. E. Lawson—
706 Pleasant St.

SANITARIUMS
Pyschean Baths—415½ Malvern

LITTLE ROCK

HOTELS
Graysonia—809 Gaines St.
New Vincent—522½ - 9th St.

TOURIST HOMES
Mrs. T. Thomas—1901 High St.

PINE BLUFF

HOTELS
P. K.—3rd & Alabama Sts
Marietta—3rd & Louisiana Sts.
Smith's—East Third St.

TOURIST HOMES
Mrs. M. J. Hollis—
1108 W. 2nd Ave.
Mrs. K. L. Bell—1111 W. 2nd Ave.

RUSSELVILLE

TOURIST HOMES
Mrs. M. Jackson—Herman St.
Mrs. E. Latimore—
318 S. Houston Ave.

TEXARKANA

HOTELS
Mrs. Conner's—W. Broad St.
Brown's—312 W. Elm St.

TOURIST HOMES
G. C. Mackey—102 E. 9th St.
Mrs. D. E. Kennedy—710 Ash St.

RESTAURANTS
Grants Cafe—830 Laurel St.

SERVICE STATIONS
Smith & Rand—723 W. 7th St.

BEAUTY PARLORS
W. B. Parlou—1020 Laurel St.

BARBER SHOPS
G. Powell—106 E. 9th St.

CALIFORNIA

BERKLEY

TAVERNS
Schaeffer's Cafe—
2940 Sacramento St.

BEAUTY PARLORS
Little Gem—1511 Russell St.

BARBER SHOPS
Success—2946 Sacramento St.

EL CENTRO

HOTELS
The Roland—201 E. Main St.

TOURIST HOMES
Mrs. L. Augustus—
420 Commercial Ave.
Emmett Terrell—193 E. Main St.

RESTAURANT
Pearl McKinney Lunch
301 Main St.

FRESNO

TRAILER PARKS & CAMPS
Barnes Drive In—1412 "F" St.

LOS ANGELES

HOTELS
Allen—1123 Central Ave.
Cark—1818 - 24 Central Ave.
Dunbar—4025 S. Central Ave.
Elite—1217 Central Ave.
Sojourner's—1119 E. Adams Blvd.
Sheridan—1824 Central Ave.
Regal—815 E. 6th St.
Arcade—542 Ceres Ave.

TOURIST HOMES
Mrs. B. Hoffman—760 W. 17th St.
Mrs. S. H. Grier—1121 E. 22nd St.
Mrs. W. D. Grealoiu—
1311 W. 35 Place

SERVICE STATIONS
The Relay—
Central Ave. at 28th St.
Lewis & Hayes—
3426 S. Central Ave.

TAVERNS
Marble Inn-1820 Imperial Highway

BEAUTY PARLORS
Mrs. A. B. Dunbar—906 E. 54th St.

LIQUOR STORES
House of Morgan—2729 S. Central

OAKLAND

TOURIST HOMES
Mrs. A. C. Clark—805 Linden St.
Mrs. H. Williams—814 Linden St.

SERVICE STATIONS
Summes'—1258 - 7th St.
McCabe—5901 Adeline St.
Signal—800 Center St.

GARAGES
Bufford's—5901 Aldine St.

TAVERNS
Overland Cafe—1719 - 7th St.
Rythm Buffet—1704 - 7th St.

BEAUTY PARLORS
Personality—3613 San Dablo Ave.

PASADENA

TAVERNS
Kentucky—1067 N. Fair Oaks

SERVICE STATIONS
Penn's Super—1285 Lincoln Ave.

SAN BERNARDINO

TOURIST HOMES
Mrs. A. Phillips—964 6th St.
S. M. Carlton—939 W. 6th St.

SAN DIEGO

HOTELS
Douglass—206 Market St.
Simmons—542 Sixth Ave.

TOURIST HOMES
Mrs. E. Wallace—537 13th St.
Mrs. M. Chance—279 "A" St.
Mrs. M. Gooden—3030 Franklin St.

RESTAURANT
Johnson's—18 N. 30th St.

SAN FRANCISCO

HOTELS
Turpin-Powell & Market Sts.

TOURIST HOMES
Mrs. L. E. Davis—1564 Jones St.
Mrs. F. Johnson—1788 Sutter St.
Helen's Guest House—1951 Sutter
Mrs. R. Hulsey—2946 Pine St.

TAVERNS
Jacks'—1931 Sutter St.

BEAUTY PARLORS
Adrian—1930 Sutter St.
Arineica's—1928 Fillmore St.
Fredonia's—1953 Sutter St.

DRUG STORES
Riggans'—2600 Sutter St.

NIGHT CLUBS
Town Club—1963 Sutter St.

SANTA MONICA

TAVERNS
La Nobita—1807 Belmount Place

TULARE

TAVERNS
Kings—322 South "K" St.

COLORADO

COLORADO SPRINGS

TOURIST HOMES
Mrs. N. Hamilton—
717 N. Corona St.
Dr. I. Moore—738 N. Spruce St.
Mrs. G. Roberts—
418 E. Cucharras St.

DENVER

HOTELS
Arapahoe—2247 Arapahoe St.
Herndon—2716 Welton St.
Rossonian—2650 Welton St.
The Ritz—2721 Welton St.

TOURIST HOMES
Mrs. M. F. Stell—2427 Ogden St.
Mrs. J. McClure—
2849 Lafayette St.
Mrs. W. Graham-2544 Emerson St.
Mrs. R. B. Anderson—
2421 Ogden St.
Mrs. A. L. Fisher—
2356 Humboldt St.

SERVICE STATIONS
Auto Service—817 E. 26 Ave.

TAXICABS
Ritz Cab Co.—2723 Walton St.

GREELEY

TOURIST HOMES
Mrs. E. Alexander—106 E. 12th St.
Rev. W. H. Mance—104 E. 12th St.

LA JUNTA

TOURIST HOMES
Mrs. R. Mitchell—322 W. 1st St.
Mrs. M. Moore—301 Lewis Ave.
Mrs. H. Tittsworth—
325 Maple Ave.

PUEBLO

HOTELS
Perry—231 S. Victoria St.
Protho House—
188 Central Main St.

TOURIST HOMES
Mrs. T. Protho—918 E. Evans Ave.
C. Forehand—1003 Spruce St.
The Roneoak—
121 E. Northern Ave.

TRINIDAD

TOURIST HOMES
Mrs. C. Brooks—114 W. 3rd St.

CONNECTICUT

BRIDGEPORT

TOURIST HOMES
Mrs. M. Barrett—83 Summer St.
Mrs. E. Lawrence—68 Fulton St.

HARTFORD

HOTELS
Log Cabin Cottage—2016 Main St.
Mme. S. A. Reed—12 Canton St.
Parrish Rooming House—
26 Walnut St.

TOURIST HOMES
Mrs. Johnson—2016 Main St.

RESTAURANT
Mitchell's—1758 Main St.

BARBER SHOPS
Parlor—1978 Main St.

BEAUTY SHOPS
Quality—1762 Main St.

TAVERNS
The Turf Club—Main St.

NEW HAVEN

HOTELS
Hotel Portsmouth—91 Webster St.
Phyllis Wheatley Home—
108 Canal St.

TOURIST HOMES
Dr. M. F. Allen—65 Dixwell Ave.
Mrs. S. Robinson—54 Dixwell Ave.
Mrs. C. Raine—68 Dixwell Ave.

RESTAURANT
Mrs. Griggs—146 Dixwell Ave.

BEAUTY PARLORS
Mme Ruby—175 Goffe St.
Harris—138 Goffe St.

SCHOOL OF BEAUTY CULTURE
Modern—170 Goffe St.

NEW LONDON

TOURIST HOMES
Home of the Bachelor—
20 Brewer St.
Mrs. Wm. Gambles—45 Shapley St.
Hempstead Cottage—
73 Hempstead St.
Mrs. E. Whittle—785 Bank St.

STAMFORD

HOTELS
Gladstone—Gay St.

TOURIST HOMES
Robert Graham—37 Hanrahan Ave.

WATERBURY

HOTELS
Jones—64 Bishop St.

TOURIST HOMES
Mrs. J. Carter—57 Bishop St.
Mrs. A. Dunham—208 Bridge St
Community House—81 Pearl St.
Mrs. B. Smith—56 Pearl St.

WEST HAVEN

TAVERNS
Hoot Owl—374 Beach St.

DELAWARE

DOVER

HOTELS
Cannon's Hotel—Kirkwood St.
Cannon's—Division St.
Caleb Brown—Lincoln St.
Dean's—Forrest St.
Moseley's—Division St.
Weston's—Division St.
The Bells—Lincoln St.

WILMINGTON

TOURIST HOMES
Mrs. E. W. America—
1106 Tatnall St.
Mrs. G. Cooper—110 W. 12th St.
Mrs. E. Till—1008 French St.
Mrs. M. Wilson—1317 Tatnall St.

BARBER SHOPS
Burton's—8th & Walnut St.

DISTRICT OF COLUMBIA

WASHINGTON

HOTELS
Henry Hotel—1825 13th St. N. W.
Johnson Hotel—1502 13th St. N. W.
Mid City—7th & N St. N. W.
Whitelaw—13th & T St. N. W.
Y. M. C. A.—1816 12th St. N. W.
Y. W. C. A.—
901 Rhode Island Ave. N. W.
J. Y's—16 "G" St. N. W.

TOURIST HOMES
Mrs. L. O. Diggs—
215 Florida Ave. N. W.
Mrs. M. J. Hines—
1929 13th St. N. W.
Mrs. R. Lee—1212 Girad St. N. W.
Mrs. E. H. Watson—
1435 "Q" St. N. W.

TAVERNS
Liberty—910 5th St. N. W.
Harrison's Cafe—
455 Florida Ave. N. W.
Service Grill—12th & V Sts. N. W.

RESTAURANTS
Key's—7th & 'T' St. N. W.
Royal Crown—1826-7th St. N. W.

BEAUTY PARLORS
Apex—1417 'U' St. N. W.
Royal Place—1629 "U" St. N. W.
The Royal—1800 "T" St. N. W.

GARAGES
University—Rear 1019 Columbia Rd. W.

SERVICE STATIONS
Brown's—Georgia Ave. & "V" St.
B. Barker—Florida Ave. & 8th St.

TAXICABS
Dixie Cab Co.—653 N St. N. W.
Brabnic Bus Service—
1102 U St. N. W.

COUNTRY CLUBS
Grossland's

NIGHT CLUBS
Caverns—11th & "U" Sts. N. W.
Republic Gardens—1355 "U" St. N. W.

FLORIDA

JACKSONVILLE

HOTELS
Blue Chip Hotel—514 Broad St.
Hotel Sanders—636 W. Ashley St.
Richmond Hotel—422 Broad St.

TOURIST HOMES
Mrs. E. H. Flipper—
739 W. Church St.
Mrs. L. D. Jefferson—
2140 Moncrief St.
Mrs. B. Robinson—
128 Orange St.
Mrs. G. L. Martin—
702 W. Beaver St.
Mrs. A. Holmes—232 W. State St.
Alpine Cottage—
714 W. Ashley St.
Mrs. C. H. Simmons
434 W. Ashley St.

LAKE CITY

TOURIST HOMES
B. J. Jones—714 E. Leon St.
L. M. Spears—
426 E. Washington St.

LAKELAND

TOURIST HOMES
Mrs. A. Davis—513 W. First St.
Mrs. J. Boyd—Missouri Ave.
Mrs. J. Gordon—
336½ N. Florida Ave.
Mrs. M. C. McCarter—
W. Pear St.

MIAMI

HOTELS
Caldwell—
Dorsey Hotel—941 N. W. 2nd Ave.
Mary Elizabeth 700 N. W. 2nd Ave.

PENSACOLA

HOTELS
Hotel Belmont—
311 N. Tarragonia St.

SEBRING

RESTAURANTS
Brown's—406 Lemon St.

ST. AUGUSTINE

TOURIST HOMES
F. H. Kelley—83 Bridge St.
H. G. Tye Apts.—132 Central Ave.

ST. PETERSBURG

TOURIST HOMES
Mrs. J. A. Barrett 28th St. & 6th Ave. S.
Mrs. C. A. Sanders 1505 5th Ave.
J. A. Bailey—942 3rd Ave. S.

TAMPA

HOTELS
Beatrice Hotel—1515 Central Ave.
Central Hotel—1028 Central Ave.
Dallas Hotel—829 Zack St.
Delux Hotel—822Contant St.

GEORGIA

ALBANY

TOURIST HOMES
Mrs. A. J. Ross 514 Mercer St.
Mrs. A. Bentley 525 Mercer St.
Mrs. L. Davis 313 South St.
Mrs. C. Washington—228 S. Jackson St.

ATLANTA

HOTELS
Mack—548 Bedford Pl. N. E.
Roosevelt—239 Auburn Ave.
Hotel Shaw—245 Auburn Ave.
James Hotel—241 Auburn Ave. N.E
McKay Hotel—Auburn Ave.
Butler Y. M. C. A.—22 Butler St.

RESTAURANT
Mrs. Suttons 312 Auburn Ave. N. E
Dew Drop Inn 11 Ashby St. N. W

TAVERNS
Yeah Man—256 Auburn Ave.

BARBER SHOPS
Artistic 55 Decatur St.

BEAUTY PARLORS
Poro Auburn & Belle St. N. E.

NIGHT CLUBS
The Top Hat—Auburn Ave. N. E
Club Royal—250 Auburn Ave.

SERVICE STATIONS
Harden's—848 Hunter St. S. W.
Flanagan's—Auburn Ave. Cor. Belle.
Halls Auburn Ave. N. E.

AUGUSTA

WINE & LIQUOR STORES
Bollingers—1114 Gwennett St.

BRUNSWICK

TOURIST HOMES
The Palms—1309 Glouster St.

COLUMBUS

HOTELS
Lowes—724—5th Ave.

DUBLIN

TOURIST HOMES
Mrs. M. Burden, 508 McCall St.
Mrs. R. Hunter 504 S. Jefferson
Mrs. M. Kea 405 S. Jefferson St.

EASTMAN

TOURIST HOMES
J. P. Cooper 211 College St.
Mrs. M. Mariano 408 1st Ave.

GREENSBORO

TOURIST HOMES
Mrs. C. Brown Cannen Section
Mrs. E. Jeter Railroad Sec.
Mrs. B. Walker Springfield Sec.

MACON

HOTELS
Douglas Hotel—361-3 Broadway
Richmond Hotel—319 Broadway

TOURIST HOMES
Mrs. M. Clemons 104 Spring St.
Mrs. E. C. Moore 122 Spring St.
Mrs. F. W. Henndon—139-1st Ave.
Mrs. C. A. Monroe 108 Spring St.

SAVANNAH

(TRAILERS PARK)
Cocoanut Grove—Mrs. J. Cox

RESTAURANT
Dreamland—43rd & Hopkins St.

SERVICE STATIONS
Oliver's—Wayne & Broad Sts.

DRUG STORES
Moores'—37th & Florence St.

BEAUTY PARLORS
Rudies'—1827 Ogeechee Road
Rose—348 Price St.

SCHOOL OF BEAUTY CULTURE
456 Montgomery St.

TAILORS
Halls—1014 W. Broad St.

WAY CROSS

TOURIST HOMES
Mrs. E. Duggar 964 Renolds St.
Mrs. K. G. Scarlett 843 Reynolds

ILLINOIS

CHICAGO

HOTELS
Brookmont—3953 S. Michigan Ave.
Grand—5048 S.Parkway
Monogram—649 E. 37th St.
Huntington—649 E. 37th St.
Southway—6018 Parkway
Tyson—4259 S. Parkway
Vincennes—601 E. 36th St.
Y. M. C. A.—3763 S. Wabash Ave.
Y. W. C. A.—4559 S. Parkway
Franklin—3942 Indiana Ave.
Lincoln—2901 State St.
Pompeii—20 E. 31st St.
Grand—51st St. & Grand Bl'v'd
New Hazle—3910 Indiana Ave.
Clarilge—51st & Michigan Ave.

TOURIST HOMES
Mabel Bank—712 E. 44 St.

RESTAURANTS
Morris'—410 E. 47 St.
Asia—3542 Michigan Ave.

GARAGES
Blackman's—4320 Inliana Ave.

SERVICE STATIONS
Turner's—
N. E. Cor. 59 St. & Wabash Ave.
Parkway—5036 S. Parkway
Waterford's—6000 S. Wabash Ave.
Standard—Garfield & S. Parkway
Balls— 70 E. 36th St.
American Giants—
5900 S. Wabash Ave.

DRUG STORES
Partee—4458 Cottage Grove Ave.

TAVERNS
The Palm—466 E. 47th St.
Coldstone's—4801 Indiana Ave.

BEAUTY PARLORS
Louis—4850 Forestvell Ave.
Matties'—4212 Cottage Grove Ave.

BARBER SHOPS
Tiptons'—5509 S. Michigan Ave.

CENTRALIA

TOURIST HOMES

Mrs. E. B. CLAYBORNE
303 N. PINE STREET

Mrs. E. Crawford—303 N. Pine St.
Mrs. B. Vernon—448 N. Poplar St.
Mrs. M. Ricks—131 N. Pine St.
Rooms for Tourists—520 N. Locust St.

MRS. MABLE COLEMAN
503 N. POPLAR AVE.

BARBER SHOPS
P. Coleman 503 N. Poplar St.

BEAUTY PARLORS
M. Coleman 503 N. Poplar St.

SERVICE STATIONS
Langenfield 120 N. Poplar St.

DANVILLE

TOURIST HOMES
Stewart—E. North St.
Mrs. G. Wheeler—109 Hayes St.
Mrs. C. Vance—1007 Harmon Ave.
Mrs. F. Newberry
412 E. Van Buren St.

EAST ST. LOUIS

HOTELS
Royal—2005 Missouri Ave.

TOURIST HOMES
Irene Yancy—1914 Bond Ave.
P. B. Reeves—1803 Bond Ave.
W. E. Officer—2200 Missouri Ave.

SPRINGFIELD

HOTELS
Dudley—130 S. 11th St.

TOURIST HOMES
Mrs. B. Mosby-1614 E. Jackson St.
Mrs. H. Robbins—
1616 E. Jackson St.
Mrs. M. Rollins—1127 E. Mason St.
Mrs. M. E. Rollins—
1123 E. Adams St.
Mrs. G. Bell—625 N. 2nd St.
Mrs. E. Brooks—705 N. 2nd St.
Dr. Ware—
1520 E. Washington St.

OTTAWA

TOURIST HOMES
Mrs. G. Danile—605 S. 3rd Ave.

ROCKFORD

HOTELS
Briggs—429 So. Court St.

TOURIST HOMES
Mrs. C. Gorum—301 Stewart Ave.
Mrs. G. Wright—422 S. Court St.
A. M. Ross—126 Chamberlain St.
S. Westbrooke—310 Olive St.

WAUKEGAN

TOURIST HOMES
Mrs. R. Norwood—819 Mott Ave.

IDAHO

POCATELLO

TOURIST HOMES
A.M.E. Parsnage—
625 E. Fremont St.
Tourist Park—E. Fremont St.

INDIANA

ANDERSON

TAVERNS
Terrance Cafe—1411 Madison Ave.

ANGOLA

Fox Lake Resort—
1½ miles S. W. of Angola

ELKHART

TOURIST HOMES
Miss E. Botts—336 St. Joe St.

EVANSVILLE

TOURIST HOMES
Mrs. B. Bell—672 Lincoln Ave.
Mrs. A. W. Lauderdale—
605 Oak St.
Miss F. Snow—719 Oak St.
The Community Center—
618 Cherry St.

FORT WAYNE

RESTAURANT
Leo Manuals'—1329 Lafayette St.

GARY

HOTELS
States'—1700 Washington St.

FRENCH LICK

HOTELS
Thurman—222 Indiana Ave.

INDIANAPOLIS

HOTELS
Morrison's—524 N. West St.

TOURIST HOMES
Morris Fur. Rms.—518 N. West St.
Neatly Fur. Rms.—330 N. Missouri St.
Mrs. E. P. Waters—
914 N. California St.
Mrs. C. Willis—
542 N. California St.
Mrs. L. Lewis—2717 Paris Ave.
Mrs. B. Farrell—928 N. West St.
Mrs. Mary Harris—924 N. West St.

RESTAURANTS
Lasley's—510 Indiana Ave.

TAVERNS
Mayes Cafe—503 Indiana Ave.
Hambric Cafe—510 Indiana Ave.

GARAGES
25th St. Gar.—553 W. 25th St.

BEAUTY PARLORS
Petite—420 W. Michigan St.

JEFFERSONVILLE

TOURIST HOMES
Charles Thomas-607 Missouri Ave.
Leonard Redd—711 Missouri Ave.

KOKOMO

TOURIST HOMES
Mrs. C. W. Winburn—
1015 N. Kennedy St.
Mrs. Chas. Hardinson—
812 N. Kennedy St.
Mrs. A. Woods-1107 N. Purdun St.
Mrs. S. D. Hughes—
1045 N. Kennedy St.

LAFAYETTE

TAVERNS
Pekin Cafe—1624 Salem St.

MARION

RESTAURANTS
Marika—416 S. Branson Ave.
Sorosis Tea Room—
405 W. 10th St.

MICHIGAN CITY

TOURIST HOMES
Allens'—210 E. 2nd St.

MUNCIE

RESTAURANT
Cozy Lunch—224 E. 2nd St.

NEW ALBANY

TOURIST HOMES
J. D. Clay—513 Pearl St.
Mrs. E. Huggins—514 Stats St.
Dr. E. R. Gaddie—
2235 E. Market St.

SOUTH BEND

RESTAURANT
Smoke's Place—432 Chapin St.

TERRE HAUTE

HOTELS
Booker—306 Cherry St.
TAVERNS
Dreamand Cafe—306 Cherry St.

WEST BADEN

HOTELS
Waddy—

EVANSVILLE

TOURIST HOMES
Z. Knight—410 S. E. 9th St.

IOWA

CEDAR RAPIDS

TOURIST HOMES
Mrs. W. H. Lavelle-812 9th Ave. E

DES MOINES

HOTELS
Marguerite—1410 Central Ave.

DUBUQUE

TOURIST HOMES
Mrs. H. Pelkey—712 Julien Ave.
Mrs. P. Martin—712 Julien Ave.
R. Brown—795 Roberts St.

OTTUMWA

TOURIST HOMES
Mrs. J. Rose—802 N. Fellows
William Bailey 526 Center Ave.
J. H. Hewitt—512 Grant
Harry Owens—814 W. Pershing

WATERLOO

TOURIST HOMES
Mrs. B. F. Tredwell—709 Logan St.
Mrs. Spencer—220 Sumner St.
Mrs. E. Lee—745 Vinton St.

KANSAS

COFFEYVILLE

TOURIST HOMES
P. C. Allen—716 E. 5th St.

CONCORDIA

TOURIST HOMES
Mrs. W. A. Crews
1st & Republican Sts.
Mrs. B. J. Johnson—102 E. 2nd St.
Mrs. Geo Smith—5th & Lincon
Mrs. Glen McVey—328 East St.

DODGE CITY

TOURIST HOMES
Mrs. Sadie Graves—911 Ave. 8th

FORT SCOTT

HOTELS
Hall's—223½ E. Wall St.
TOURIST HOMES
Peter Thomasun—
114 S. Ransom St.

HIAWATHA

TOURIST HOMES
C. Saunders—
202 Pottawottamie St.
Mrs. Mary Saunders—
1014 Shawnee

HUTCHINSON

TOURIST HOMES
Mrs. C. Lewis—400 W. Sherman
Mrs. Lucy Monroe—21 F. West

INDEPENDENCE

TOURIST HOMES
Major McBee—418 S. 3rd St.
Mrs. A. Peak—613 S. Penn St.

JUNCTION CITY

HOTELS
Bridgeforth—311 E. 11th St.
Cottery—1120 N. Washington St.
TOURIST HOMES
Mrs. B. Jones—229 E. 14th St.

LARNED

TOURIST HOMES
Mrs. C. M. Madison—828 W. 12 St.
Mrs. Mose Madison—518 W. 10 St.
Mrs. John Caro
E. 6th St. & Johnson Ave.

LAURENCE

HOTELS
Snowden's—1933 Tennessee St.

LEAVENWORTH

TOURIST HOMES
Mrs. W. Shelton—223 Linn St.
Mrs. J. Hamiton—720 N. 3rd St.
W. D. Stewart—809 N. 4th St.

KANSAS CITY

BEAUTY PARLORS
Katurah's—433 Qundoro St.
Baskin's—1935 N. 5th St.

MANHATTAN

TOURIST HOMES
Mrs. E. Dawson—1010 Yuma St.
Mrs. H. Jackson—830 Yuma St.

OTTAWA

TOURIST HOMES
Rev. John Allen—211 E. Logan St.
Mrs. Marie Clayborne—
502 E. 2nd St.
Mrs. Folson—112 N. Poplar
Mrs. R. W. White—821 Cypress

PARSONS

TOURIST HOMES
Mrs. F. Williams—
2216 Grand Ave.

TOPEKA

HOTELS
Dunbar—400 Quincy St.

TOURIST HOMES
Mrs. E. Slaughter—1407 Monroe
Elks Community Center—
1504 Adams St.

TAVERNS
Mack's—400 Quincy St.
Power's Cafe—116 E. 4th St.

WICHITA

HOTELS
Oklahoma House—517½ N.
Main St.

RESTAURANTS
Oklahoma Cafe—517 N. Main St.

KENTUCKY

ELIZABETHTOWN

TOURIST HOMES
Mrs. Bettie Board—N. Mile St.
A. Johnson— Valley Creek Road
Mrs. M. B. Tyler—Mile St.
M. E. Wintersmith-S. Dixie Ave.

GLASCOW JUNCTION

HOTELS
Preston—

HAZARD

TOURIST HOMES
Mrs. J. Razor—436 E. Main St.
Mrs. Jessie Richardson

HOPKINSVILLE

TOURIST HOMES
Mrs. M. McGregor-200 E. First St.
L. McNary—113 Liberty St.
J. C. Hopkins— 128 Liberty St.

LOUISVILLE

HOTELS
Allen—2516 W. Madison St.
Pythian Temple—
10th & Chestnut Sts.
Walnut—615 Walnut St.
Y. W. C. A.—528 S. Walnut St.

TOURIST HOMES
Lucy A. Brown—1012 W. Chestnut
Hattie Daniels—
1512 W. Chestnut

RESTAURANTS
Butler-Roberts—654 S. 10 St.

GARAGES
Eade's—2420 Cedar St.

BEAUTY PARLORS
Bellonia—1625 Callagher St.
Verona—1428 W. Walnut St.

BARBER SHOPS
Hunter's—1501 W. Chestnut St.

LEXINGTON

RESTAURANTS
The Abbey Food Shop—
374 E. 3rd St.

MT. STERLING

HOTELS
Dew Drop Inn—E. Locust St.

TOURIST HOMES
Mrs. E. Butler—133 E. Locust St.
Mrs. G. White—131 E. Locust St.
Mrs. G. Grubbs—1562 E. High St.

PADUCAH

HOTELS
Jefferson's—514 S. 8th St.
Metropoltian—724 Jackson St.

TOURIST HOMES
W. T. Carter—709 Washington
S. M. Bacon—1203 Clay
R. Blakemore—902 Washington
R. Bard—918 N. 10th
Mrs. N. E. Boyd—1009 N. 10th St.
Humble's—408 S. 8th St.

LOUISIANA

BATON ROUGE

HOTELS
Ever-Ready—1236 Louisiana Ave

TOURIST HOMES
T. Harrison—1236 Louisiana Ave.
RESTAURANTS
Ideal Cafeteria—1501 E. Blvd.
TAVERNS
Waldo's—864 S. 13th St.
BEAUTY PARLORS
Carrie's—570 S. 13th St.
BARBER SHOPS
Malacher's—1341 Government St.
SERVICE STATIONS

HORATIO'S ESSO SERVICE
1150 SOUTH BOULEVARD

NIGHT CLUBS
Paradise—220 Boatnes St.
ROAD HOUSES
Apex Club—Louise St.

BOGALUSA

TOURIST HOMES
Mrs. E. L. Raine—508 North Ave.
Mrs. R. Spellman Bennett—
501 Ave. S.

LAFAYETTE

TOURIST HOMES
Mrs. L. B. Hebert—618 Clay St.
Mrs. A. Miles—302 John St.
J. Bondreaux—315 Stewart St.

MANSFIELD

TOURIST HOMES
S. A. Wilson—N. Jefferson St.
W. Simpkins—Jenkins St.
M. Biles—Crosby Sub-division

MONROE

TOURIST HOMES
Turner's—11th & Desiard
R. H. Burns—700 Adams
L. B. Hortons—Congo St.

MORGAN CITY

TOURIST HOMES
Mrs. L. Williams-719 Federal Ave.
Mrs. N. Green—First St.
Mrs. E. White—302 Third St.
Mrs. V. Williams—208 Union St.

NEW ORLEANS

HOTELS
Astoria—225 S. Rampart St.
Patterson—761 S. Rampart St.
The Chicago—1310 Iberville St.
Paige—1038 Dryades Ave.
Riley—759 S. Rampart St.
Palace—1834 Annette St.

TOURIST HOMES
Mrs. F. Livaudais—
1954 Jackson Ave.
N. J. Bailey—2426 Jackson Ave.
Mrs. P. Hart—1725 Iberville St.
Mrs. King—2826 Louisiana Ave.
TAVERNS
John's Cafe—
Felicity & Howard Sts.
Green Parrot—1050 Rampart St.
RESTAURANTS
French Coffee Pot—
2931 Magnolia St.
BARBER SHOPS
1800 Dryades Ave.
Elk's—2818 La Salle St.
BEAUTY PARLORS
Golden Green—2500 Magnolia St.
SERVICE STATIONS

BILL BOARD ESSO SERVICE
So. Claiborne & 6th St.

TAXICABS
V-8 Cab Line—
Felicity & Howard Sts.

NEW IBERIA

TOURIST HOMES
M. Robertson—116 Hopkins St.
Mrs. C. Vital—201 Frenzel St.
N. E. Cooper—913 Providence St.

OPELOUSAS

TOURIST HOMES
V. Arceneaux—723 E. Landry
H. Johnson—N. Market St.
B. Giron—S. Lonbard St.

SHREVEPORT

TOURIST HOMES
Grant Flats—1239 Reynolds
Mrs. J. Jones—1950 Hotchkiss
Mrs. A. Webb—1245 Reynolds
Mrs. W. Elder—1920 Hotchkiss

MAINE

AUGUSTA

TOURIST HOMES
Mrs. J. E. McLean—16 Drew St.

BANGOR

TOURIST HOMES
Mrs. L. Elms—118 Parker St.

PORTLAND

HOTELS
The Thomas House—28 "A" St.

TOURIST HOMES
Mrs. E. D. Richey-84 Congress St.

MARYLAND

ANNAPOLIS

HOTELS
Wright's—26 Calvert St.

NIGHT CLUBS
Washington—61 Washington St.

BALTIMORE

HOTELS
Smith's—
Druid Hill Ave. & Paca St.
York—1200 Madison Ave.
Clark—Dolphin & Marison Ave.
Hawkins—902 Madison Ave.
Majestic—1602 McColloh St.
Penn—1631 Pennsylvania Ave.
Stokes—1500 Argyle Ave.
Reed—1002 McCulloh St.
Y. M. C. A.—1600 Druid Hill Ave.
Y. W. C. A.—1200 Druid Hill Ave.

RESTAURANTS
Gorden's—1533 Druid Hill Ave.
Murry's—1522 Penn Ave.
Spot Bar-B-Q—1530 Penn Ave.

BEAUTY SHOPS
M. King—1510 Penn Ave.
Scott's—1526 Penn Ave.
La Banch—1527 Penn Ave.

BARBER SHOPS
Nottingham—1619 Penn Ave.

TAVERNS
Velma—Cor. Penn. & Bake St.
The Alhabra—1520 Penn. Ave.
Wagon Wheel—1638 Penn. Ave.

NIGHT CLUBS
Ubangi—2413 Penn. Ave.
Little Comedy—1418 Penn. Ave.

GOLF CLUBS
Monumental—14 E. Pleasant St.

GARAGES
Jacks'—514 Wilson St.

CEDAR HEIGHTS

NIGHT CLUBS
Hill Top Inn

FREDERICK

TOURIST HOMES
Mrs. J. Makel 119 E. 5th St.
Mrs. W. W. Roberts 316 W. South
E. W. Grinage 22 W. All Saints

RESTAURANTS
Crescent—16 W. All Saints St.

HAGERSTOWN

TOURIST HOMES
Frank Long—Jonathan St.
Harmon—226 N. Jonathan St.

MARLBORO

HOTELS
Wilson

SALISBURY

TOURIST HOMES
M. L. Parker 110 Delaware Ave.

MASSACHUSETTS

ATTLEBORO

TOURIST HOMES
J. R. Brooks Jr.—54 James St.

BOSTON

HOTELS
Harriett Tubman—25 Holyoke St.
Melbourne—815 Tremont St.
Mothers Lunch—510 Columbus Ave.

TOURIST HOMES
Mrs. Holeman—
212 W. Springfied St.
Mrs. M. Johnson—
616 Columbus Ave.
Ancrum S. Dormitories—
74 W. Rutland Sq.
Mrs. E. A. Taylor—
192 W. Springfield St.
Mrs. Ford—209 W. Springfield St.

RESTAURANTS
Julia Walters—912 Tremont St.
Estelles'—888 Tremont St.
Slade's Bar-b-que—
958 Tremont St.
Western Lunch Box—431 Mass. Ave.

BEAUTY PARLORS

MRS. W. J. WILLIAMS
62 HAMMOND ST.

Clark-Merrill—505 Shawmut Ave.
Amy's—796 Tremont St.
Peoples—678 Shawmut Ave.
Geneva's—808 Tremont Ave.
Estelle's—15 Greenwich Ave.
Mme. F. S. Blake—363 Mass. Ave.
E. L. Crosby—11 Greenwich Park
Mme. Enslow's—977 Tremont St.
Victory—46 W. Canton St.
E. West—609 Columbus Ave.

TAXICABS
Robt. A. Robinson—
41 Monroe St.

GARAGES
DePrest—255 Northampton

GREAT BARRINGTON

TOURIST HOMES
Mrs. I. Anderson—28 Rossiter St.

HYAMIS

TOURIST HOMES
Zilphas Cottages—134 Oakneck Rd.

ROAD HOUSES
Guwmars—188 Goswold St.

NORTH ADAMS

TOURIST HOMES
F. Adams—32 Washington Ave.

NEEDHAM

TOURIST HOMES
B. Chapman—799 Central Ave.

PITTSFIELD

TOURIST HOMES
M. E. Grant—53 King St.
Mrs. T. Dillard—109 Linden St.
Mrs. B. Jones—50 W. Union St.
Mrs. C. Cummings—47 N. John St.
Mrs. B. Jasper—66 Dewey Ave.
J. Marshall—124 Danforth Ave.

PLYMOUTH

TOURIST HOMES
Mrs. Taylor—11 Oak St.
W. A. Gray—47 Davis St.

ROXBURY

TOURIST HOMES
Mrs. S. Gale—168 Townsend St.

BEAUTY PARLORS
Aberleen—45 Bower
Mme. Lovett—68 Humbolt Ave.

TAXICABS
Harvey Thompson—82 Monroe

SPRINGFIELD

TOURIST HOMES
Mrs. M. E. Gillum—58 - 7th St.
Mrs. Sheppard—171 King St.

TAILORS
Amercian Cleaners—
433 Eastern Ave.

SWAMPSCOTT

TOURIST HOMES
Mrs. M. Home—3 Boynton St.

MICHIGAN

ANN ARBOR

HOTELS
American-123 W. Washington St.
Allenel—126 El Huron St.

TOURIST HOMES
Mrs. E. M. Dickson—144 Hill St.

BALDWIN

SERVICE STATIONS
Bayak's-J. Morgan, Prop.
Nolph's Super Service

BATTLE CREEK

TOURIST HOMES
Mrs. L. Dennis—10 Oak St.
Mrs. F. Brown—76 Walters Ave.
Mrs. P. Grayson—22 Willow
Mrs. C. S. Walker—
709 W. Van Buren

BENTON HARBOR

NIGHT CLUBS
Research Pleasure Club—
362 8th St.

BITELY

HOTELS
Kelsonia Inn—R. R. No. 1
Royal Breeze—on State Route 37

DETROIT

HOTELS
Biltmore—1926 St. Antoine St.
Dunbar—550 E. Adams St.
Tansey—2474 Antoine St.
Eizabeth—413 E. Elizabeth St.
Fox—715 Madison St.
Le Grande—1365 Lafayette St.
Norwood—550E. Adams St.
Northcross—
St. Antoine & Columbia
Russell—615 E. Adams St.
Preyer—2476 St. Antonie St.
Dewey—505 E. Adams St.
Davidson—556 E. Forest Ave.

BEAUTY PARLORS
Cleo's—4848 Hastings St.

SERVICE STATION
Cobb's Maple & Chene Sts.

AUTOMOBILES
Davis Motor Co.
421 E. Vernon H'way

DRUG STORES
M. Dorsay—2201 St. Antoine St.
Aztec—5001 S. State St.

FLINT

TOURIST HOMES
T. Kelley—407 Wellington Ave.
T. L. Wheeler—1512 Liberty St.
Mrs. F. Taylor—1615 Clifford St.

HARTFORD

TOURIST HOMES
Mrs. R. E. J. Wilson—210 E. 4th

IDLEWILD

HOTELS
Eagles Nest
Hickory Inn
Indian Inn
Idlewild Island
Oakmere-on the Island

TOURIST HOMES
Edinburgh Cottage—Miss Herrone
N. Kenner
B. Riddles
Forest Inn-Miss. Schuler, Prop.
Meadow Lark Haven—Pine St.

RESTAURANTS
Lorine Lunch—Baldwin Rd.
Busy Bee Chicken Shack
The Rosana—Mrs. Brown, Prop.

TAVERNS
Busy Bee Tavern & Luncheon

BEAUTY PARLORS
Alexis Beauty Parlor

BARBER SHOPS
C. Henderson

GARAGES
N. R. Williams

JACKSON

TOURIST HOMES
Mrs. W. Harrison—
1215 Greenwood Ave.
Mrs. N. Jones—222 E. Franklin
Mrs. S. Collins—1211 Woodbridge

LANSING

TOURIST HOMES
M. Busher—1212 W. St. Joe St.
Mrs. M. Gray—1216 W. St. Joe St.
Mrs. Lewis—816 S. Butler St.
Mrs. Cook—1220 W. St. Joe St.
Mrs. J. B. Gains—1406 Albert St.

MUSKEGON

TOURIST HOMES
R. C. Merrick—
65 E. Muskegon Ave.
Rev. Fowler—937 McIlwraigh St
R. A. Swift—472 W. Monroe

SAGINAW

TOURIST HOMES
Mrs. M. Gant—312 S. Baum St.
Mrs. J. Curtley—439 N. Third St
Mrs. P. Burnette-406 Emerson St

MINNESOTA

DULUTH

TOURIST HOMES
Mrs. C. Colby—616 E. 4th St.

MINNEAPOLIS

HOTELS
Serville—246½—4th Ave. So.

TOURIST HOMES
Phyllis Wheatley House—
809 Aldrich N.

ST. PAUL

TOURIST HOMES
Reuben Floyd—379 Carroll St.

RESTAURANTS
G. & G. Bar-B-Q—318 Rondo St.

MISSISSIPPI

BILOXI

TOURIST HOMES
Mrs. L. Scott—421 Washington St.
Mrs. G. Bess—624 Main St.
Mrs. M. Pickens—616 Main St.
A. Alcina—437 Washington St.

CHARLESTON

TOURIST HOMES
C. Pollard—Rear Court Square

COLUMBUS

HOTELS
Queen City—15th St. & 7th Ave.

TOURIST HOMES
Mrs. L. Alexander—N. 12th St.
H. Sommerville-906 N. 14th St.
Mrs. I. Roberts—
12th St. & 5th Ave. N.
M. J. Harrison—917 N. 14th St.

GREENVILLE

TOURIST HOMES
Mrs. B. B. Clark—508 Ohea St.

GRENADA

TOURIST HOMES
Mrs. K. D. Fisher—72 Adams St.
Mrs. F. Williams—
H'way 51 & Fairground R.
Henry's Lodge—
H'way 51 & Fairground R.

HATTIESBURG

TOURIST HOMES
W. A. Godbolt—409 E. 7th St.
Mrs. A. Crosby—413 E. 6th St.
Mrs. S. Vann—636 Mobile St.

LAUREL

HOTELS
Bass—S. Pine St.
TOURIST HOMES
John Reed—E. First St.
Mrs. A. Wilson—607 S. 7th
Mrs. S. Lawrence—902 Meridian
Mrs. E. L. Brown—522 E. Kingston
Mrs. F. Garner—
909 Joe Wheeler's Ave.
Mrs. S. G. Wilson—802 S. 7th

MACOMB

HOTELS
Townsend—534 Summit St.
TOURIST HOMES
D. Mason—218 Denwidde St.

MERIDIAN

HOTELS
Beales—2411 Fifth St.
TOURIST HOMES
Mrs. H. Waters— 1201 26th Ave.
Mrs. M. Simmons—
5 St. bet. 16 & 17 Aves.
Charley Leigh—5 St. & 16th Ave.

NEW ALBANY

HOTELS
Foot's—Railroad Ave.
TOURIST HOMES
S. Drewery—Church St.
Patt Knox—Cleveland St.
C. Morganfield—Cleveland St.

VICKSBURG

TOURIST HOMES
Mrs. B. V. Foote— 913 1st St.

YAZOO CITY

HOTELS
Caldwell—Water & Broadway Sts.
TOURIST HOMES
Mrs. C. A. Wright—234 S. Yazoo
Mrs. A. J. Walker—321 S. Monroe
Mrs. H. Lattimore-Washington St

MISSOURI

CAPE GIRARDEAU

TOURIST HOMES
G. Williams—408 S. Frederick St.
W. Martin—38 N. Hanover St.
J. Randol—422 North St.

CARTHAGE

TOURIST HOMES
Mrs. M. Webb—S. Fulton St.
Mrs. A. Peal—E. Third St.
Mrs. A. Gibson—
Bois De Arc & 5 St.

COLUMBIA

TOURIST HOMES
Mrs. B. Smith—608 Park Ave.
Mrs. W. Harvey—417 N. 3rd

CHARLESTON

TAVERNS
Creole Cafe—311 Elm St.

EXCELSIOR SPRINGS

HOTELS
The Albany—408 South St.

JEFFERSON CITY

HOTELS
Lincoln—600 Lafayette St.

JOPLIN

HOTELS
Williams—308 Pennsylvania St.
TOURIST HOMES
J. Lindsay—1702 Pennsylvania St.
Mrs. A. G. Tutt—812 West "A" St.

KANSAS CITY

HOTELS
Booker T.—Vine St. & 18th St.
Street's—1508 E. 18th St.
Watson—1211 S. Highland St.
Cadillac—15th & Forest

TOURIST HOMES
Mrs. K. F. Bell—2146 E. 24th St.
Mrs. I. Fairfax—1914 E. 24th St.

BEAUTY PARLORS
EUthola—1602 E. 19th St.
Modern—1815 Vine St.

LEBANON

TOURIST HOMES
Mrs. J. Osborne—Route 3
Mrs. Ann Wilson—Route 3
Mrs. Missorui Warfield—Route 3
Mrs. Eliza Turner—Route 3

MOBERLY

TOURIST HOMES
Mrs. F. Davis—212 N. Ault St.
Mrs. F. Gunn—529 Winchhester St.
Ralph Bass—517 Winchester St.
W. Johnson—N. 5th St. 400 blk.

POPLAR BLUFF

TOURIST HOMES
A. L. Davis—426 Short Oak St.
Mrs. W. Brooks—1800 N. Alice St.
D. C. Freeman—720 Margrett St.

SEDALIA

TOURIST HOMES
Mrs. T. L. Moore—505 W. Cooper
Mrs. C. Walker—217 E. Morgan
W. Williams—317 E. Johnson

SPRINGFIELD

TOURIST HOMES
U. G. Hardrick—238 Dollison Ave.
Allen's Rms.—638 N. Jefferson St.

ST. JOSEPH

TOURIST HOMES
Mrs. T. J. Coleman—
1713 Angelique St.
Mrs. I. Scott—2203 Sylvannie St.
Mrs. H. K. Williams—
202 E. Nebraska St.

ST. LOUIS

HOTELS
Booker T. Washington—
Jefferson & Pine
Poro College—
Pendleton & St. Ferdinand
West End—
W. Belle & Vandevanter Sts.
Grand Central—Jefferson & Pine

RESTAURANTS
Oak Leaf—4269 W. Easton Ave.

BEAUTY PARLORS
Allen's—2343 Market St.
Moore's—3334 Franklin Ave.

BARBER SHOPS
Bullock's—3320 Franklin Ave.

SERVICE STATIONS
Fred Cooper's—Pine at Ewing Ave
Brook's—1918 Pendleton

GARAGES
Davis—3811 Finney Ave.

MONTANA

HELENA

TOURIST HOMES
Mrs. M. Stitt—204 S. Park

NEBRASKA

FREMONT

TOURIST HOMES
Mrs. C. M. Brannon—
1550 N. "C" St.
Gus Herndon—1725 N. Irving St.

HASTINGS

TOURIST HOMES
Mrs. T. Mose—902 S. Kansas Ave.

LINCOLN

HOTELS
Tourist Camp—27th & Saltillo

TOURIST HOMES
Mrs. W. R. Colley—1035 Rose St.
Mrs.R. Johnson—907 "S" St.
Mrs. E. Edwards—2420 "P" St.

OMAHA

HOTELS
Broadview—2060 N. 19th St.
Patton—1014—18 S. 11th St.

TOURIST HOMES
L. Sirawther—2220 Willis Ave.
Mrs. M. Smith—2211 Ohio St.
Miss. W. M. Anderson—
2207 N. 25th St.
G. H. Ashby—2228 Wilis Ave.
Dave Brown—2619 Caldwell St.

NEW JERSEY

ASBURY PARK

HOTELS
Metropolitan—
1200 Springwood Ave.
Whitelead—25 Atkins Ave.
Reevy's—135 De Witt Ave.
Adore—104 Myrtle Ave.

TOURIST HOMES
Mrs. A. Arch—23 Atkins Ave.
Mrs. E. C. Burgess—
1200 Springwood Ave.
Mrs. W. Greenlow—
1317 Summerfield Ave.

Mrs. M. Wigfall—1112 Adams Ave.
Mrs. Brown—135 Ridge Ave.
Mrs. C. Jones—141 Sylvan Ave.
Mrs. V. Maupin—25 Atkins Ave.
Mrs. Minyard—1106 Adams Ave.
Mrs. S. Wilks—1112 Mattison Ave.
E. C. Yesger—1406 Mattison Ave.
Anna Eaton—23 Adkins Ave.

SANITARIUMS
Parks Rest.—115 DeWitt Ave.

RESTAURANTS
Danny's—Springwood Ave.
George's—159 Springwood Ave.
West Side—1136 Springwood Ave.
Nellie Fritts—Springwood Ave.
Helen's Carolina—
1200 Springwood A.

TAVERNS
Aztex Room—1147 Springwood Ave.
Capitol—1212 Springwood Ave.
Hollywood—1318 Springwood Ave.
2 Door—1512 Springwood Ave.

SERVICE STATIONS
Johnson—
Springwood & Dewitt Pl.

GARAGES
Arrington—153 Ridge Ave.
West Side—1206 Springwood Ave.

BARBER SHOPS
Consolidated—
1216 Springwood Ave.
John Milby—1216 Springwood Ave.

BEAUTY PARLORS
Imperial—1107 Springwood Ave.
Opal—1146 Springwood Ave.
Wilie's—37 Sylvan Ave.
Marion's—1119 Springwood Ave.

NIGHTS CLUBS
Jeffs'—1208 Springwod Ave.

ROAD HOUSES
Perry's—Route 33

TAXICABS
Nomath—1130 Adams St.

ATLANTIC CITY

HOTELS
Bay State—334 N. Tennessee Ave.
Liberty Apt.—
Baltic & Kentucky Ave.
Randell— 1601 Arctic Ave.
Ridley—1806 Arctic Ave.
Swan—136 Virginia Ave. N.
Wright—1702 Arctic Ave.
Capitol—37 N. Kentucky Ave.
Lincoln—911 N. Indiana Ave.
Luzon—601 N. Ohio Ave.

TOURIST HOMES
Mrs. V. Jones—1720 Arctic Ave.
Mrs. R. Diggs—1825 Wash. Ave.
P. Tanner—110 N. Indiana Ave
M. Contee— 111 N. Indiana Ave.
R. Dowling—328 N. Indiana Ave.

TOURIST HOMES

SATCHELL'S COTTAGE
27 N. MICHIGAN AVE.

A. R. S. Goss—
324 N. Indiana Ave.

RESTAURANTS
Goldens'—41 N. Kentucky Ave.
Little Diner—
104 N. Kentucky Ave.

TAVERNS
Goldens'—41 N. Kentucky Ave.
Austins—
Maryland & Baltic Aves.
My Own— Delaware & Artic Ave.
Little Belmont—
37 N. Kentucky Ave.
Elks Bar & Grill—
1613 Arctic Ave.
Wonder Bar—
Kent & Arctic Aves.
Timbuctu—1608 Arctic Ave.

NIGHT CLUBS
Paradise—N. Illinois Ave.
Harlem—32 N. Kentucky Ave.

BARBER SHOPS
42 N. Illinois Ave.
Hollywood—811 Arctic Ave.

BEAUTY PARLORS
Graces'—43 Kentucky Ave.

WINE & LIQUOR STORES
Goodmans—1317 Arctic Ave.
Macks—New York & Baltic Aves.
Tumble Inn—
Delaware & Baltic Aves.

DRUG STORES
London's—
Cor. Kent & Arctic Aves.

ATLANTIC HIGHLANDS

RESTAURANTS
Tennis Club Tea Room—
Prospect Ave.

BAYONNE

TAVERNS
Doc's—67 W. 23rd St.

BRIDGESTON

TAVERNS
The Ram's Inn—
Bridgeston & Millville Pike

CAMDEN

TAVERNS
Jack's—245 Chestnut St.

TAILORS
Economy—818 Kaign Ave.
Merchant—741 Kaign Ave.

CAPE MAY

HOTELS
De Griff—830 Corgie St.
Richardson—Jackson St.

TOURIST HOMES
Mrs. S. Giles—806 Corgie St.
Mrs. M. Green—728 Lafayette St.

CEDAR KNOLL

COUNTRY CLUBS
The Shady Oak Lodge

EAST ORANGE

BEAUTY PARLORS
Matties—186 Amherst St.
Ritz—276 Main St.
Milans—232 Halsted St.

TAILORS
Vernon's—182 Amherst St.
Charles—63 N. Park St.

EATONTOWN

NIGHT CLUBS
The Greenbrier—Pine Bush

ROAD HOUSES
Bob Jones Cottage—Pine Brook

EGG HARBOR

HOTELS
Allen House—
625 Cincinnati Ave.

SERVICE STATIONS
Walker's—154 Cincinnati Ave.

TAVERNS
Red, White & Blue Inn—
701 Phil Ave.

ELIZABETH

TOURIST HOMES
Mrs. L. G. Brown—173 Madison St.
Mrs. T. T. Davis—27 Dayton St.
Mrs. G. Pierson—1093 Williams St.
Mrs. J. Pryde—1125 Fanny St.

RESTAURANTS
Paradise—1129 E. Grand St.

TAVERNS
Hunter's—1155 Dickerson St.
One & Only—1112 Dickerson St.

ENGLEWOOD

LIQUOR STORES
Giles—107 Williams St.

TAVERNS
The Lincoln—13 Englewood Ave.

GARAGES
Dwight's Garage—25 So. Van Brunt St.

HACKENSACK

BARBER SHOPS
Central Service—174 Central Ave.
Dotson—234 1st St.

BEAUTY PARLORS
Mary—206 Central Ave.

TAVERNS
Rideouts Bar—204 Central Ave.

HASKELL

RECREATION PARKS
Thomas Lake

KINGSTON

ROAD HOUSES
Merrill's

JERSEY CITY

RESTAURANTS
Rogers'—54 Kearney Ave.

KEYPORT

RESTAURANTS
Hargrave Community Sandwich Shoppe

KENNELWORTH

TAVERNS
Drivers'—17th & Monroe Ave.

LAWNSIDE

HOTELS
Hi-Hat Inn—Whitehorse Pike

TAVERNS
Acorn Inn—Whitehorse Pike
Dreamland
La Belle Inn—Gloucester Ave.

RECREATION PARKS
Lawnside Park

LINDEN

NIGHT CLUBS
4th Ward Club—
1035 Baltimore Ave.

LONG BRANCH

RESTAURANTS
The Main Stem—163 Belmont Ave.
TAVERNS
Club "45"—Liberty St.
Cosmopolitan—192 Belhont Ave.
Sam Hall—18 Academy St.
Tally-Ho—185 Belmont Ave.

MAGNOLIA

TAVERNS
Green's

MADISON

TAXICABS
Yellow—14 Lincoln Place

MONTCLAIR

RESTAURANTS
J. & M.—213 Bloomfield Ave.
NIGHT CLUBS
Recreation—Glenridge Cor. Bay
SCHOOL OF BEAUTY CULTURE
Hair Dressing—207 Bloomfield Ave.
BARBER SHOPS
Paramount—211 Bloomfield Ave.
GARAGES
Maple Ave.—80 Maple Ave.

MORRISTOWN

TAVERNS
Spring Gardens—135 Spring St.
NIGHT CLUBS
Eureka—118 Spring St.

NEWARK

HOTELS
Grand—78 W. Market St.
TOURIST HOMES
Mrs. M. Johnson—
151 Pennslyvania Ave.
Mrs. E. Morris—39 Chester Ave.
Mrs. Spence—506 Washington St.
RESTAURANTS
Dixie Chicken Club—
178 Orange St.
Royal Palm—123 Waverly Ave.
TAVERNS
Alcaza—72 Waverly Pl.
Bert's—174 W. Kinny St.
Charles—125 Broome St.
Dan's—245 Academy St.
Dodgers—8 Bedford Pl.
Little Jonny's—47 Montgomery St.
Lestbaders—175 Spruce St.
Kesselman's—13th & Rutgers St.
Rosen's—164 Spruce St.
Daves'—202 Court St.
Reiff's—94 So. Orange Ave.
Rim Tim Inn—179 Orange St.
Saul's—60 Waverly Ave.
The Hi Spot—173 W. Kinny St.
Warren & Norfolk—256 Warren St.
Woods—258 Prinnce St.
Kleinbergs—88 Waverly St.
BARBER SHOPS
El Idelio—28 Wright St.
Teals—137 Somerset St.
BEAUTY PARLORS
Gomes—230 W. Kinny St.
La Vogue—227 W. Kinny St.
Irene's—125 Somerset St.
Farrar—35 Prince St.
Billys'—202 Belmont Ave.
Chapmans'—96 Belmont Ave.
Jeanette—105½ W. Market St.
NIGHT CLUBS
Boston Plaza—4 Boston St.
Golden Inn—150 Charleston St.
Nest Club—Warren & Newark St.
New Kinny Club—36 Arlington St.
Villa Maurice—375 Washington St.
AUTOMOTIVE
Dixons' Auto Painting—
106 Charlton St.

ORANGE

HOTELS
Oakwood Dep't—84 Oakland Ave.
RESTAURANTS
Triangle—152 Parrow St.
Presto—6 Main St.
Marie—148 Central Place
Jeter's—77 Parrow St.
CHINESE RESTAURANTS
Orange Gardens—132 Parrow St.
NIGHT CLUBS
Deve & Manney's Paradise—
Parrow & Chestnut Pl.
Forth—Second—157 Parrow St.
TAVERNS
Frank's—120 Hickory St.
TAILORS
Fitchitt—99 Oakwood Ave.
Triangle—101 Hickory St.
DRUG STORES
Bynum & Catlette—
Parrow & Hickory Sts.

OCEAN CITY

HOTELS
Comfort—2-1 Bay Ave.

PATERSON

HOTELS
Joymakers—38 Bridge St.

RESTAURANTS
Governor—130 Governor St.

TAVERNS
Idle Hour Bar—53 Bridge St.
Abes'—98 Straight St.
Joymakers—38 Bridge St.

BARBER SHOPS
Johnsons—130 Governor St.

BEAUTY PARLORS
Jimmies—581 E. 18th St.

GARAGES
Browns'—57 Godwin St.

PERTH AMBOY

BARBER SHOP
Kellys'—128 Fayette St.

POINT PLEASANT

TAVERNS
Joe's—337 Railroad Ave.

PRINCETON

TOURIST HOMES
Mrs. Gregory—28 Green St.

RESTAURANTS
Grigg's—58-60 Witherspoon St.

PLAINFIELD

TAVERNS
Liberty—4th St.

RED BANK

RESTAURANTS
Vincents Dining Room—
263 Shewsbury Ave.

TAVERNS
West Bergen—103 W. Bergen Pl.

BARBER SHOPS
A. Dillard—250 Shewsbury Ave.

BEAUTY PARLORS
R. Alleyne—124 W. Bergen Pl.
Surles—214 Shewsbury Ave.

SERVICE STATION
Galatres—Shewsbury & Catherine

TAILORS
Dudley's—79 Sunset Ave.

ROSELLE

TAVERNS
Alpha Bar—302 E. 9th St.
St. George—
1139 St. George Ave.

SCOTCH PLAINS

RESTAURANTS
Hill Top—60 Jerusalem Road

ROAD HOUSES
Villa Casanova—Jerusalem Road

COUNTRY CLUBS
Shady Rest Jerusalem Road

SEA BRIGHT

RESTAURANTS
Essie Kings—11 New St.

TRENTON

TOURIST HOMES
A. W. Hurley—26 Barnes St.
Mrs. M. Morris—116 Spring St.
Mrs. P. Cash—88 Spring St.
Mrs. Garland—62 Spring St.

VAUX HALL

BEAUTY PARLORS
Celeste—211 Springwood Ave.

TAVERNS
Carnegie—380 Carnegie Place

ROAD HOUSES
Lloyd Chicken Farm—
26 Valley St.

WEST PLEASANTVILLE

COUNTRY CLUBS
Pine Acres—

WILDWOOD

HOTELS
Glen Oak—100 E. Lincoln St.
The Marion—
Arctic & Spicer Aves.
The Poindexter—
106 E. Schellenger Ave.

TOURIST HOMES
The Denmond-129 W. Spicer Ave.
Mrs. G. Stenson—107 W. Roberts
Mrs. A. H. Brown—3811 Arctic
Mrs. E. Crawley—3816 Arctic
Mrs. J. Quarles—106 Cedar

NEW YORK STATE

ALBANY

TOURIST HOMES
Mrs. M. C. Williams—18 Ten Broeck Pl.
Mrs. I. Dorsey—25 Second St.
Mrs. Adams—216 Hamilton St.
Mrs. G. Bedell—23 Second St.
Mrs. C. Madison—391 Orange St.
Mrs. A. J. Oliver—42 Spring St.

BUFFALO

HOTELS
Francis—Exchange St.
Little Harlem—494 Michigan Ave.
Montgomery—486 Michigan Ave.
Vendome—177 Clinton St.

TOURIST HOMES
Mrs. F. Washington— 172 Clinton
Mrs. G. Chase—192 Clinton
Wm. Campbell—22 Milnor

BROOKLYN

TOURIST HOMES
Mrs. A. E. Bryan—156 Leffets Pl.

RESTAURANTS
Dew Drop—363 Halsey St.
M. & M.—1455 Fulton St.
Richardson—1686 Fulton St.
Rosebud—1081 Fulton St.
El Rose—1093 Fulton St.
Little Roxy—490-A Summer Ave.

TAVERNS
Royal—1073 Fulton St.
Utopia—1093 Fulton St.
Goodwill—1942 Fulton St.
Parkside—759 Gates Ave.

WINES & LIQUOR STORES
Yak—1361 Fulton St.

NIGHT CLUBS
Hanlew—334 Lewis St.
Lion's—307 Ralph Ave.

BEAUTY PARLORS
Bartleys—1125 Fulton St.
Lamae—545 Classon Ave.
Cloverleaf—425 Gates Ave.
Diddy's—1518 Fulton St.
Emma's—1391 Fulton St.
La. Roberts—285 Grand Ave.

SCHOOLS OF BEAUTY CULTURE
J. K.—417 Tompkins Ave.
Ritz—1358 Fulton St.
Theresa—304 Livonia Ave.

LONG ISLAND

CORONA

TAVERNS
Big George—106 Northern Blvd.
Prosperity—32-19—103rd St.

FREEPORT

NIGHT CLUBS
Cotton Inn—77 E. Sunrise Highway

HEMPSTEAD

TAVERNS
Eddie's—28 S. Franklin St.

WESTBURY

TAVERNS
Josh's—635 Union Ave.

WESTCHESTER

ELMSFORD

TAVERNS
Clarke, 91 Saw Mill River Road

NEW ROCHELLE

RESTAURANTS
Betsy Ann, 442 North Ave.
City Park, 521 5th Ave.
Harris, 29 Morris St.
Rogers, 50 Winyah
Week's, 68 Winyah

TAVERNS
Bal-Mo-Ral, 56 Brook St.

NIGHT CLUBS
Sky Vue, Wingah & Brook St.

BEAUTY PARLORS
A. Berry, 50 DeWitts Pl.
B. Miller, 8 Brook Ave.
H. Johnson, 97 Winthrop Ave.
Maion's, 108 Winthrop Ave.
Ocie, 41 Rochelle Pl.
Orchid, 57 Winyah Ave.

BARBER SHOPS
The Royal Salon, 4 Brook Ave.
Field's—66 Winyah Ave.

PHARMACY
Daniel's—57 Winyah Ave.

LARCHMONT

TAVERNS
Park, 1 5th Ave.

The Green Book is always ready

To Serve You

Use it on each trip

Patronize these Listed Places

SOUTHWARD

Chas. A. R. McDowell
Collaborator
United States Travel Bureau

A daylight ride on a Greyhound bus from New York to Washington does not present any scenic wonders, yet it pays to keep one's eyes open. Our strongest impression arises from the contrast between the beautiful, flower surrounded plants of General Motors and Burnett's Gin at Linden, New Jersey; and the immense drab, abandoned industrial plants along the Delaware River at Marcus Hook and vicinity where thousands of workers once labored and lived, but never saw any beauty of any sort.

Unless absolutely necessary, the traveler should never pass through Washington without stopping, if for only a few hours. This procedure always leaves us "soothed and sustained." At this time to such an extent that we could leave at midnight for an eighteen hour ride to Greenville, S. C. which took us through the heart of the tobacco country, and the cities of Richmond, Danville, Winston-Salem and Charlotte. Our object in visiting Greenville was to meet with the Colored Business and Professional Men's Club. This organization is thoroughly interested in creating a nation-wide interest in travel. The result of this meeting was very encouraging. There was a large attendance and close attention was paid to our remarks. A number of questions were asked, which brought on a hearty discussion. Greenville lays claim to being the Textile Center of the South. We note, with special interest the Negro community, the Hight School, the excellent hospital facilities and many beautiful homes, owned by Negroes.

The 164 mile ride through well terraced farm lands and peach orchards to Atlanta, was highly enjoyable. Atlanta is entered through the suburbs of Decatur and the beautiful Ponce de Leon Avenue. Decatur Street in Atlanta, Beale Street in Memphis, and Yamacraw in Savannah have been made famous by Negroes. It was our good fortune after many years to be able to visit Decatur Street on Saturday night, don't miss this, if you ever go to Atlanta. Atlanta is the center of high education for Negroes, and here is located the Atlanta Daily World, the only Negro daily newspaper in the United States. After a good night's rest at the Butler Street Y. M. C. A., we began our Sunday ride 294 miles on the old Central and Georgia Railroad (over General Sherman's route to the sea).

At Savannah we visited Irene Mound, about 5½ miles above the City on Pipemakers Creek. For over two years, the Government has been uncovering this pre-historic Indian village. This work is being done under the direction of Dr. Hooten of Harvard University and Dr. Caldwell is the archaeologist in charge. A laboratory and a museum have been established at this site and a large number of Negro W. P. A. workers is employed. The Mound is in a dense growth of live oakes and the scenery is superb.

"Savannah has been acclaimed by famous world travelers, as one of the most beautiful cities in the world and its rich background and heritage of history, embracing many events notable in American annals, provide it with many hollowed spots of deepest interest to the visitor." On route 17 just south of the City, of unique interest, is Cocoanut Grove. Here we find a modern tourist camp, amusement pavilion and the beautiful home of Mrs. Mamie Cox, maid of the late Miss Marie Dressler, famous in the movies. All of this was provided through funds left to Mrs. Cox by Miss Dressler, with the stipulation that she would build a suitable place for the comfort of Negro travelers.

A little further back, we referred to Yamacraw in Savannah. Here is located a magnifiicent old colonial building, First Bryan Baptist Church, founded in 1788, and one of the oldest Negro churches in North America. According to information furnished by the pastor, this Church is soon to become the focal point around which the new governmnet housing project is to be constructed.

Anyone visiting Savannah between April 1st and October 1st, should by all means take the ride on the steamer among sea islands and through the various inlets to Beaufort, S. C. The round trip consumes about 12 hours. Most of the scenery is wild and primitive, and all of it is beautiful. The cost for the round trip is one dollar. Soon after boarding the steamer for this trip, we noticed a Colored man, exercising much authority. Crossing Port Royal Sound (the only rough water on the trip) looking up at the pilot house, we noticed this man at the wheel, looking ahead and calmly smoking his cigar, a sight seldom seen elsewhere. Negroes have long been associated with navigation in South Carolina waters.

(CONTINUED ON PAGE 31)

MT. VERNON

ROAD HOUSES
Pitts, 24 W. 3rd St.
Mohawk Inn, 142 S. 7th Ave.

SCHOOL OF BEAUTY CULTURE
Okeh, 224 S. 7th Ave.
Orchid, 48 W. 3rd St.

OSSINING

ROAD HOUSES
Goodie Shop, 51 Hunter St.

TARRYTOWN

TAVERNS
Bridge Rendezvous—
40 Cortland St.

NORTH TARRYTOWN

BARBER SHOPS
Lemon's, Valley St.
J. Brown, Valley St.

BEAUTY PARLOR
J. Prioleau, 88 Valley St.

TUCKAHOE

RESTAURANTS
Major's, 48 Washington St.
Butterfly Inn, 47 Washington St.

BARBER SHOPS
Al's, 144 Main St.

BEAUTY PARLORS
Shahana, 144 Main St.

WHITE PLAINS

RESTAURANTS
Goody Shop, Brookfield St.
Lloyd's—88 Martine Ave.

TAVERNS
Oasis, 115 Tarrytown Road

BEAUTY PARLORS
Marie's, 94 Brookfield St.

NEW YORK CITY

HOTELS
The Viola—227 West 135th St.
The Tenrub—328 St. Nicholas Ave.
El-Melrah—21 West 135th St.
Martha—6 West 135th St.
Elks—608 St. Nicholas Ave.
Garrett House—314 West 127th St.
Douglas—809 St. Nicholas Ave.
Beakford—300 West 116th St.
Adrienne—2053—7th Ave.
Braddock—126th St. & 8th Ave.
Dewey Square—201 W. 117th St.
Fane-Dumas—205 West 135th St.
Grampion—182 St. Nicholas Ave.
Olga—695 Lenox Ave.
Press—23 West 135th St.
The Harreit—271 West 127th St.
Woodside—2424—7th Ave.
Currie—101 West 145th St.
Theresa—125th St. & 7th Ave.

RESTAURANTS
Aunt Dinah's Kitchen—
172 West 135th St.
Clara's Kitchen—275 St. Nich. Ave.
Edgecombe Rotisserie—
431 Edgecomb Ave.
Ideal—247 West 145th St.
Jimmie's Chicken Shack—
763 St. Nicholas Ave.
Craig's—55 St. Nicholas Place.
Little Gray Shop—2465—7th Ave.
Garland's—266 West 145th St.
Lou's Kitchen—2297—7th Ave.
Millicent's—826 St. Nicholas Ave.
Pete's—2534—8th Ave.
Southern—2201—7th Ave.
Tillie's—227 Lenox Ave.
Virginia—271 West 119th St.

TAVERNS
Bowman's Grill—773 St. Nich. Ave.
Village Inn—2204—5th Ave.
Old Time Tavern—2160—5th Ave.
International—2150—5th Ave.
Dore's—2163—5th Ave.
Arthur's—2481—8th Ave.
Big Apple—2300—7th Ave.
Bird Cage—2308—7th Ave.
Blue Heaven—378 Lenox Ave.
Brittwood—594 Lenox Ave.
Calvacade—2104—7th Ave.
Chick's—148th St. & 7th Ave.
Colonial Krazy House—116
Bradhurst Ave.
Eddie's—714 St. Nicholas Ave.
Elk Scene—469 Lenox Ave.
Heat Wave—1991—7th Ave.
Hot-Cha—2280—7th Ave.
Jay's—400 West 148th St.
La Mar Cheri—739 St. Nich. Ave.
Logas—2496—7th Ave.
Moon Glow—220 West 145th St.
Monte Carlo—2247—7th Ave.
Murrain—635 Lenox Ave.
Orange Blossom—570 Lenox Ave.
Pedro Montanez—22 Lenox Ave.
Speedway—92 St. Nicholas Place
Swanee—218 St. Nicholas Ave.
Victoria—2418—7th Ave.
721 St. Nicholas Ave. Grill.
Borderline—7 West 116th St.
Fat Man—St. Nicholas Ave. & 145th St.
Wellsworth's—*Cor.* 126 St. & 7th Ave.

GARAGES
Viaduct—101 Macombs Place.
Colonial Park—310 West 144th St.

BEAUTY PARLORS
- Bee's—202 West 130th St.
- Josephine's—202 St. Nicholas Ave.
- Myers & Griffin—65 W. 134th St.
- Your Pal—222 West 133rd St.
- National—301 West 144th St.
- Frances—2446—7th Ave.
- Cottie's—165 West 127th St.
- Neuway—143 West 116th St.
- Millicent—301 West 141st St.
- A. L. Smith—2411—7th Ave.
- Oneda's—231 Edgecombe Ave.
- Sibley's—301 West 126th St.
- Edna's—75 St. Nicholas Place.
- Beard's—322 St. Nicholas Ave.

AUTOMOTIVES

NIGHT CLUBS
- Small's Paradise—2294—7th Ave.
- Capitol—115 Lenox Ave.
- Elks Rendezvous—133rd St. Lenox Avenue.
- Harlem Hollywood—105 W. 116 St.
- Vincent's—2120 Madison Ave.

SCHOOL OF BEAUTY CULTURE
- Apex—200 West 135th St.
- Mme. C. J. Walker—239 W. 125 St.

AUTO LOANS
- Community—2368—7th Ave.

DANCE HALLS
- Savoy—Lenox Ave. & 140th St.
- Goldn Gate—Lenox Ave. 142 St.

TAILORS
- La Fontaine—470 Convent Ave.
- Little Alpha—84 West 120th St.
- L. D. Colley—100 W. 134th St.

MILLINERY
- Beulah's—296 Manhattan Ave.
- Ira's—2441—7th Ave.

HABERDASHER
- James—2255—7th Ave.

ROOM SERVICE
- Serv-U—805 St. Nich. Ave. Apt. 24

ROAD HOUSES
- Speedway Gardens—31 Dykeman St.

BARBER SHOPS

FERRY AND TUNNEL RATES FOR PASSENGER CARS.

Holland Tunnel 50c
George Washington Bridge 50c
Lincoln Tunnel 50c
Electric Ferry—42nd St. 25c
Dyckman St. Ferry 25c
Yonkers Ferry 50c
125 St. Ferry 25c

Tri-Boro-Bridge from New York City to Worlds' Fair and points in Long Island 25c

Henry Hudson Bridge on Express Highway going north 10c

KEY TO STREET NUMBERS IN MANHATTAN

To find what street is nearest, take the street numer, cancel last figure, divide by 2, add or subtract key number found below. The result will be the nearest street.

Ave. A .... Add 3
Ave. B .... Add 3
Ave. C .... Add 3
Ave. D .... Add 3
1st Ave .... Add 3
2nd Ave. .... Add 3
3rd Ave. .... Add 9 or 10
4th Ave. .... Add 8
5th Ave.
  Up to 200 .... Add 13
  Up to 400 .... Add 16
  Up to 600 .... Add 18
  Up to 775 .... Add 20
  Above 2000 .... Add 24
6th Ave. .... Subt. 12 or 13
7th Ave. .... Add 12
8th Ave. .... Add 9 or 10
9th Ave. .... Add 13
10th Ave. .... Add 14
11th Ave. .... Add 15
Amsterdam .... Add 59 or 60
Audubon .... Add 165
Columbus .... Add 59 or 60
Convent .... Add 127
Edgecombe .... Add 134
Ft. Washington .... Add 158
Lenox .... Add 110
Lexington .... Add 22
Madison .... Add 26
Manhattan .... Add 100
Park .... Add 34 or 35
Pleasant .... Add 101
St. Nicholas .... Add 110
Wadsworth .... Add 173
West End .... Add 59 or 60
B'way ab. 23. Subt. 30 or 31

Central Pak West—Divide house number by 10 and add 60.

Riverside Drive—Divide house number by 10 and add 72.

Streets—To find nearest avenue, count 100 numbers to the block, east or west

Here in Beaufort is a large house, formerly the home of Robert A. Small, (Negro) the famous blockade runner of the Civil War. At Fort Pulaski National Monument, at the mouth of the Savannah River, we find what is probably the largest fig tree in the world. It has a spread of 170 feet. It is 32 feet high and the yearly average production is 50 bushels of figs. Thirteen miles south of the City of Savannah is located the United States Department of Agriculture Bamboo propagation farm, and a short distance further at Ways Station, Georgia, Mr. Henry Ford has established his 70,000 acre model community. We learned of the friendly interest he has shown in Cocoanut Grove.

Speeding north through Dixie, you do not open the coach windows now for a breath of air and an eyeful of cinders. On a curve, every now and then, we could glance ahead through the clear glass and see the Seaboard's huge yellow diesel "on the job". How different!

AUTOMOTIVES

- Savoy Tire Shop—612 Lenox Ave.
- J. Jones—120 West 145th St.
- Andy Radiator—416 West 127th St.
- A. Eastmond—31 West 144th St.
- C. Jones—25 East 136th St.
- Daly Bros.—485 St. Nicholas Ave.
- Green's Auto—110 West 145th St.
- L. Martinez—612 Lenox Ave.
- Meisel Tire—2079—7th Ave.
- Nathan Auto Parts—34 W. 145 St.
- Simons Supply—133 W. 145th St.
- Ullman & Hauser—27 St. Claire Pl.
- W. J. McAvoy—703 Lenox Ave.
- Gordon Seale—155 W. 145th St.

BARBER SHOPS

- Renaissance—2349—7th Ave.
- Delux—2799—8th Ave.
- World's Fair—251 W. 145th St.
- Bob Cary's—2521—8th Ave.
- Spooner's—2435—8th Ave.
- A. McCargo—242 West 145th St.
- B. Garrett—2311—7th Ave.
- Eldorado—203 West 116th St.
- Esquire—2265—7th Ave.
- Hi-Hat—2276—7th Ave.
- Hoghie Rayford—2013—7th Ave.
- H. Parks—200 West 146th St.
- Latin American—2395—8th Ave.
- Leon & Teddy's—353 W. 145th St.
- Lud—166 West 116th St.
- Park Lane—2206—7th Ave.
- Manhattan—2456—8th Ave.
- Majestic—130 West 116th St.
- Modernistic—2132—7th Ave.
- Roxy—2322—7th Ave.
- Royal—749 St. Nicholas Ave.
- Edean—237 West 145th St.
- World—2621—8th Ave.

RADIO SERVICE

- Joe's—15 West 133rd St.

WINE & LIQUOR STORES

POINTS OF INTEREST IN NEW YORK CITY

THE EMPIRE STATE BUILDING is the tallest office building in the world and is situated at 5th Avenue between 33rd and 34th Streets. The site is nearly 2 acres and rises 102 stories above the ground and is 2 stories under the ground. It houses more than 25.000 tenants. Its elevators rise at the tremendous speed of 200 feet per second. While its express cars carry one to the 80th floor in one minute.

ELLIS ISLAND is the first landing place of the immigrant and is located in the upper bay of New York harbor. This island may be visited by securing a pass from the Commissioner of Immigration.

CATHEDRAL OF ST. JOHN THE DIVINE, located at Amsterdam Avenue 110th to 113th Streets, is America's greatest church edifice. When completed it will be the largest Gothic Cathedral in the world. The seating capacity is 15,000 and room for 40,000 standing. It has been in the building for the last 61 years the corner stone being laid in 1892. Visitors are always welcome and services are held practically all day.

THE GEORGE WASHINGTON BRIDGE, over the Hudson River, is the longest suspension bridge in the East, connecting New York City at 179th Street and Fort Lee. N. J. It is used by millions of people annualy, and is the Northern route to motorists going South from the North. Its towers, which stand 80 feet higher than the Washington Monument can be seen for miles around. The New York tower has the "Will Rogers Mem-orial Beacon," which serves as a guide to aviators.

THE THEATRICAL DISTRICT OF NEW YORK, where all of the largest and best plays are staged and produced, is located in the heart of the city. Here you will find the largest and best showhouses in the world from 39th to 52nd Streets and 8th to 6th Ave. ·

The colored show houses are located in Harlem: The Lafayette at 7th and 132nd Street; a W. P. A. house and the Apollo at 125th near 8th Avenue are the largest.

THE GENERAL POST OFFICE is the largest post office in the world. It covers 2 city blocks from 31st Street to 33rd and from 8th to 9th Avenue. It houses 18,000 employees, makes 26 collections and 3 to 4 deliveries a day.

THE HOLLAND TUNNEL is the busiest vehicular tunnel in the world. Starts at Canal Street in New York and ends at 12th Street, Jersey City; N. J. This tunnel contains 2 tubes: one for West bound and the other for East bound traffic; each 2 tubes wide. The toll is 5oc per car.

THE TRI-BOROUGH BRIDGE, which connects three of the boroughs of Greater New York (Manhattan, Bronx, Queens). This bridge is 17½ miles long and is the most direct route to the New York World's Fair. The toll charge is 25c.

CHINATOWN, at the Bowery and Chatham Square, is New York's Oriental section Sight seeing busses will take visitors there from Times Square. Showing the Bloody Corner at Pell and Mott Streets which has been the place of countless murders caused by the rivalry of the Leong and Hip Sing Tongs.

THE HAYDEN PLANETARIUM, which is located in the American Museum of Natural History at 81st Street and Central Park West can be seen "The Drama of the Skies." The most interesting feature of he Planetarium is the "Hall of the Sun," which shows the Solar System.There are six performances daily starting at 11 A. M. except Sunday and holidays. On these days the show starts at 10 A. M. The admission is 25c, 11 to 5 o'clock; evenings 8:30, 35c; 25c at 5 P. M. Saturday, Sunday and holidays. Children under 17 years of age 15c at all times. Reserved seats 50c and 60c.

ROCKEFELLER CENTER largest building project ever undertaken by private capital. Is situaed between 5th and 6th Avenue at 48th and 51st Streets, and occupies 12 acres. The tallest building in the group is the R. C. A. Building and is 70 stories tall and houses the National Broadcasting Co. On the West of Rockefeller Center is the Radio City Music Hall R. K. O. Building R. C A.. Building west and the Center Theatre, also Radio City which is named in honor of the Radio Corporation of America. On the Fifth Avenue side will be found the Le Maison Francaise, British Empire Building, Italian Buildng and the six story extension of the International Building.

POINTS OF INTEREST IN NEW YORK CITY

CITY HALL at Broadway, Park Row and Chambers Street. It is the seat of government of the great metropolis and can be visited by the public from 10 o'clock A. M. to 4 P. M. daily.

CENTRAL PARK, which is the largest park in the city is located at 5th Avenue and Central Park West, 59th to 110th Streets. It contains 862 acres of which is water. It is 2½ miles long and half a mile wide. It contains a Zoological Park and many play grounds.

THE AQUARIUM, located at the Battery, can be reached by all subway and elevated lines. The exhibit includes all kinds of fish, both salt and fresh water also invertebrates. Open daily: hours 9 to 5 P. .M April to September, and 9 A. M. to 4 P. M. October to March. The admission is free. The New York Aquarium is probably the largest in the world and has the largest collection of fish. It contains 7 large pools and 144 glass fronted aquarias.

COOPER UNION-MUSEUM FOR THE ARTS OF DECORATION, Cooper Square at 7th St., Open daily except Sundays, 10-5., evenings, Oct. 1- 6:30- 9:30 Except Saturdays and Sundays. Free.

CLOISTERS, The Branch of Metropolitan Museum of Art, Fort Tyron Park. Hrs: 10-5., Sundays 1-6., Closed Christmas Morning. Free except Mon. and Fri. 25c. Hrs. 8 to dusk; Sundays and Holidays 10 to dusk; Library closed on Sat., July

NEW YORK ZOOLOGICAL PARK, Bronx Park—Hrs. 10 to dusk every day. Free except Mondays and Thursday Adults 25c, Children 15c.

NEW YORK BOTANICAL GARDEN, East of 200th St., and Webster Avenue. Hrs. March 1 to November 1, 10 to 5; November to March 1, 10 to 4:30.

NEW YORK MUSEUM OF SCIENCE AND INDUSTRY, R. C. A. Bldg., Rockefeller Center. Hrs: 10 to 10 every day. Adults 25c., Children 10c.

AMERICAN MUSEUM OF NATURAL HISTORY, Central Park West at 79th St. Hrs: 9 to 5; Sunday 1 to 5. Free

AMERICAN GEOGRAPHICAL SOCIETY, Broadway at 156th St. Hrs: 9 to 4:45 Closed Sundays and Holidays: and on Saturdays during the summer.

MUSEUM OF THE CITY OF NEW YORK, Fifth Avenue at 104th St. Hrs: 10-5, Sundays 1-5. Closed Tuesdays. Free except Mondays 25c.

MUSEUM OF THE NUMISMATIC SOCIETY, Broadway between 155th- 156th Sts. Hrs: 2-5 Daily and Sundays. Closeed July 16 to Sept.. 1, Free.

MUSEUM OF THE AMERICAN INDIAN, Heye Foundation, Broadway at 155th St. Hrs. 2-5. Closed Sundays, Holidays and through July and August.

HAMILTON GRANGE, 287 Convent Avenue. Hrs: 10-5; Saturdays 10-1. Closed Sundays and Holidays. Free

WHITNEY MUSEUM OF AMERICAN ART, 10 West 8th St. Hrs. Tuesday to Friday, 1-5; Saturday and Sunday 2-6. Closed Mondays and Midsummer Months. Reopens about September 15. Free

PIERPONT MORGAN LIBRARY, 33 East 36th St. Hrs: Main Bldg., Tues. and Thusdays, 11-4; Exhibition Room, Daily 10-5. Closed Sundays, Holidays and July 1 to Sept. 7. Free.

MUSEUM OF LIVING ART, Fifth Avenue at 82nd St. Hrs.-10-5, Sundays 1-6., Closed Christmas Morning. Free except Mondays and Fridays. 25c.

FRICK COLLECTION, 1 East 70th St. Hrs., Sundays and Holidays 1-5. Closed Mondays, Decoration Day, July 4th, Month of August and Christmas. Free.

CONEY ISLAND, New York's own seaside recreation resort is ten miles from New York City. Here one will find bathing and all sorts of open air amusements.

BROOKLYN MUSEUM, Eastern Parkway and Washington Avenue, Brooklyn. Hrs: 10-5., Sundays 2-6., Free except Mon. and Fri. Adults 25c Children 10c.

BROOKLYN BOTANIC GARDEN, 1000 Washington Ave., Brooklyn; Garden Hrs. 8 to dusk; Sundays and Holidays 10 to dusk; Library closed on Sat., July 15—Sept. 15. Hrs; Mon. to Fri 9-5., Saturdays 9-12. Free.

NEW YORK STATE

ELMIRA

HOTELS
Wilson—307 E. Clinton St

TOURIST HOMES
Mrs. J. A. Wilson—
307 E. Clinton St.

JAMESTOWN

TOURIST HOMES
Mrs. I. W. Herald—51 W. 10th St.
Mrs. A. Henrick—70 W. 13th St.
Mrs. J. M. Brown—108 W. 11th St.
Mrs. C. Majors—906 Jefferson St.

KINGSTON

RESTAURANTS
Jackson Bros.—15 Cornell St.

NIAGARA FALLS

HOTELS
Rose Reta—621 Erie Ave.
Belmont Grill—447 First St.

TOURIST HOMES

The Parker House—627 Erie Ave.
Mrs. A. Scott—1015 Niagara St.

FAIRVIEW
413 MAIN ST.

Mrs. Brown—1202 Haeberle Ave.
A. E. Gabriel—635 Erie Ave.
C. A. Brown—443 Main St.

BEAUTY PARLORS
La Belle—Erie Ave.
The Parker House—627 Erie Ave.

BARBER SHOPS
Ashford—Erie Ave.
Garland—Erie Ave.

TAVERNS
Sunset Cafe—619 Erie Ave.
Chef. W. Martin— 609 Erie Ave.
Belmont Grill—447-1st St.

GARAGES
Smith & Bradberry—352—1st St.

PORT JERVIS

TOURIST HOMES
Mrs. L. Robinson—21 Bruce St.
R. Pendleton—26 Bruce St.
John Scott—28 Bruce St.

POUGHKEEPSIE

TOURIST HOMES
Mrs. R. Sullivan—14 Gregory Ave.
Mrs. S. Osterholt—16 Crannell St.
Mrs. S. Le Fever—217 Union
G. W. Hayes— 93 N. Hamilton

ROCHESTER

HOTELS
The Freeman House—
112 Industrial St.
Gibson—461 Clarissa St.
Johnson—86 Industrial St.

TOURIST HOMES
Mrs. G. W. Burks—
221 Columbia Ave.
Mrs. Latimer—179 Clarissa St.

NIGHT CLUBS
Cotton—Joseph St.

SCHENECTADY

TOURIST HOMES
R. Rhinehart—125 S. Church St.
S. Kearney—357 Vedder Ave.
G. D. Thomas- 123 S. Church St.
E. L. Claiborne—
1808 Campbell Ave.

SYRACUSE

HOTELS
Savoy—518 E. Washington St.

UTICA

TOURIST HOMES
Broad St. Inn—415 Broad St.
Mrs. S. Burns—314 Broad St.
The Howard Home—
413 Broad St.

WATERTOWN

TOURIST HOMES
E. F. Thomas—123 Union St.
V. H. Brown—502 Finase St.
G. E. Depuy—710 Morrison St.

NEW MEXICO

DEMING

TOURIST HOMES
Matt Wilson—Iron & 2nd St.

NORTH CAROLINA

ASHEVILLE

HOTELS
Booker T. Washington—409 Southside Ave.
Savoy—Eagle & Market Sts.

RESTAURANTS
Palace Grill—19 Eagle St.

BEAUTY PARLORS
Butler's—Eagle & Market Sts.

BARBER SHOPS
Wilson's—13 Eagle St.

TAVERNS
Wilson's—Eagle & Market Sts.

GARAGES
Wilkin's—Eagle & Market Sts.

CARTHAGE

HOTELS
Carthage Hotel

CHARLOTTE

HOTELS
Sanders—2nd St.

TAVERNS
Shaws' Cafe—724 Mint St.

DURHAM

HOTELS
Biltmore—E. Pettigrew St.
Jones—502 Ramsey St.

TAVERNS
Hollywood—118 S. Mangum St.

BEAUTY PARLORS
De Shazors—809 Fayetteville St.
D'Orsay—120 S. Mangum St.

SERVICE STATIONS
Midway—Pine & Poplar Sts.
Pine Street—1102 Pine St.

FAYETTEVILLE

HOTELS
Bedford Inn—203 Moore St.
Restful Inn—418 Gillespie St.

TAVERNS
Bedford Inn—203 Moore St.
Big Buster—Gillespie St.

BARBER SHOPS
Delux—Person St.

BEAUTY PARLORS
Mrs. Brown—Person St.

ELIZABETH CITY

TAVERNS

GASTONIA

HOTELS
Union Sq.

GREENSBORO

HOTELS
Travelers Inn—612 E. Market St.
Legion Club—829 E. Market St.

TOURIST HOMES
T. Daniel, 912 E. Market
Mrs. E. Evans, 906 E. Market
Mrs. Lewis—829 E. Market St.

TAVERNS
Paramount—907 E. Market St.
Roof Garden—901½ E. Market St.

TAILORS
Shoffners'—922 E. Market St.

HENDERSON

TOURIST HOMES
Mrs. Betch—219 Rockspring St.

TAXICABS
Green & Chavis—720 Eaton St.

LITTLETON

HOTELS
Youngs Hotel

MT. OLIVE

RESTAURANTS
Black Beauty Tea Room

NEW BERN

HOTELS
Rhone—42 Queen St.

TOURIST
H. C. Sparrow, 68 West St.

TAVERNS
Palm Garden—192 Broad St.

LEXINGTON

SERVICE STATIONS
D. T. Taylor—Esso Service

RALEIGH

HOTELS
Arcade
TOURIST HOMES
L. B. Yeargan— 210 E. Cabarrus
TAVERNS
Savoy—410 S. Blount St.
Joe Blacknails 407½ Blount St.

SANFORD

HOTELS
Philipps—Pearl St.

SALISBURY

TAXICABS
Safety—122 N. Lee St.

SUMTER

TAVERNS
Silver Moon—20 W. Liberty St.

WILSON

HOTELS
Biltmore—E. Washington St.
The Wilson Biltmore—539 E. Nash
TAXICABS
M. Jones—1209 E. Queen St.

WINDSOR

TOURIST HOMES
W. Payton—

WINSTON-SALEM

HOTELS
Lincoln—9 E. 3rd St.
TOURIST HOMES
Ch. H. Jones—1611 E. 14th St.
Mrs. J. Penn, 115 N. Ridge Ave.
Mrs. H. L. Christian, 302 E. 9th St.
Mrs. N. Jones, 859 N Liberty St.
R. B. Williams,
1225 N. Ridge Ave.
NIGHT CLUBS
Club 709—709 Patterson Ave.
TAXICABS
Sam Harris—6th & Patterson Ave.
Reliable—430 N. Church St.
Diamond—301 N. Church St.

WASHINGTON

DRUG STORES
Lloyd's—408 Gladden St.

WELDON

HOTELS
Pope
Terminal Inn—Washington Ave.

WILMINGTON

HOTELS
Paynes—417 N. 6th St.
TAXICABS
Tom's Taxi

OHIO

AKRON

HOTELS
Garden City—Howard & Furnace Sts.
Mathews—77 N. Howard St.
The Upperman—197 Bluff St.
Green Turtle—
Federal & Howard Sts.
TOURIST HOMES
F. Murphy's—172 Bluff St.
C. McQueen—645 Moon St.
RESTAURANTS
Check-Inn-Lunch—691 Edgewood St.
TAVERNS
Brook's—42 N. Howard St.
BEAUTY PARLORS
Beauty Salon—70 N. Howard St.
SERVICE STATIONS
Zuber's—47 Cuyahoga St.

ALLIANCE

TOURIST HOMES
Blackburn's Aparts.—
719 Keystone St.
Mrs. H. Baber-649 N. Liberty Ave.
Mrs. W. Jackson—744 N. Webb.

CANTON

TOURIST HOMES
K. S. Willis—1104 6th St. S. W.
Mrs. M. W. Smallwood—
1203 Housel St. S. E.
K. Summerville—
1104-6th St. S. W.

RESTAURANTS
Hunters—527 Cherry Ave. S. E.

BARBER SHOPS
Barbe,—525 Cherry Ave. S. E.

DRUGGIST
Southside—415 Cherry Ave. S. E.

BEAUTY PARLORS
Vanitie Shop—
528 Cherry Ave. S. E.

CINCINNATI

HOTELS
Cotton Club—
Steeling 6 & Mound Sts.
Cordella—612 N. 6th St.
Delmer—2945 Gilbert Ave.
Manse—1004 Chapel St.

TOURIST HOMES
O. Steele— 3239 Beresford Ave.

RESTAURANTS
New Candle Light—1004 Chapel St.
Uncle Lee's—1132 Chapel St.

TAVERNS
Edgemont Inn—2950 Gilbert Ave.
The Delmae—2945 Gilbert Ave.
Candle Light—1004 Chaple St.

DRUG STORES
Sky Pharmacy—5th & John St.

BARBER SHOPS
Collegiate—2982-Gilbert Ave.

BEAUTY PARLORS
Efficiency—878 Beecher
The Hosmer—920 Churchhill Ave.

CLEVLAND

HOTELS
Phyllis Wheatly—4300 Cedar Ave.
Geraldine—2212 E. 40th St.
Ward—4113 Cedar Ave.
Y. M. C. A.—E. 76th St. & Cedar
Lincoln—E. 40th St. & Scovill Ave.
Majestic—2291 E. 55th

TOURIST HOMES
Mrs. McCray—2416 E. 40th St.

BEAUTY PARLORS
Lu Zell, 2211 E. 55th St.

TAVERNS
Log Cabin—2294 E. 55th St.

SERVICE STATIONS
Sohio—E. 93rd St. & Cedar Ave.
Wrights, E. 92nd & Cedar

GARAGES
Rollin, E. 40th & Central
Sykes'—8708 Cedar Ave.

COLUMBUS

HOTELS
Fulton, 403 E. Fulton St.
Litchferd, N. 4th St.
Macon, 368 N. 20th St.
Plaza, Long St. & Hamilton Ave.
Charlton—439 Hamilton Ave.
Flints—703 E. Long St.
Kea—318½ No. 20th St.

SERVICE STATIONS
King's Shell—E. Long at Monroe
Peyton Sohio's-E. Long at Monroe

COSHOCTON

RESTAURANTS
BenWhites'—107 N. 2nd St.

DAYTON

TOURIST HOMES
B. Lawrence—206 Norwood St.

LIMA

TOURIST HOMES
Daisy Boone— 1105 W. Spring St.
Sol Downton— 1107 W. Spring St.
Edward Holt— 406 E. High St.
Amos Turner-1215 W. Spring St.
George Cook— 230 S. Union St.

LORAIN

TOURIST HOMES
B. H. Tapsico...115 W. 17th St.
Mrs. Alex Cooley—114 W. 26th
Smith's Manor—on—Erie Beach
Camp Merriman—110 W. Erie Ave.
Mrs. W. H. Redmond—201 E. 22nd
Mrs. Elishe Worthington—
209 W. 16th St.
Porter Wood— 1759 Broadway
H. P. Jackson—2383 Apple Ave.

MARIETTA

HOTELS
St. James—Butler St.

TOURIST HOMES
Mrs. E. Jackson—213 Church St

HOW TO KEEP FROM GROWING OLD

Always race with locomotive to Crossings. Engineers like it; It; breaks the monotony of their jobs.

Always pass the car ahead on curves or turns. Don't use horn, it may unnerve the fellow and cause him to turn out too far.

Demand half the road—the middle half. Insist on your rights.

Always speed; it shows them you are a man of pep even tho an amateur driver.

Never Stop, look or listen at railroad crossings. It consumes time.

Always lock your brakes when skidding. It makes the job more artistic.

In Sloppy weather drive close to pedestrians. Dry cleaners appreciate this.

Never look around when you back up; there is never anything behind you.

Drive confidently, just as tho there were not eighteen million other cars in service.

NEWARK

.TOURIST HOMES
Mrs. I. Ransom—78 Hoover St.
W. S. Hatton—22 East St

OBERLIN

HOTELS
Oberlin Inn—College & Main

SANDUSKY

TOURIST HOMES
Mrs. A. Dodd—810 Center St.

SPRINGFIELD

HOTELS
Posey, 209 S. Fountain Ave.
Y. M. C. A.—Center St:
Y. W. C. A.—Clarke St:

TOURIST HOMES
Mrs. M. E. Wilborn—220 Fair St.
Mrs. H. Sydes—
902 S. Yellow Spring St.
Mrs. C. Seward—1090 Mound St.

RESTAURANTS
The Elite—So. Center St.

NIGHT CLUBS
The Elks—So. Yellow Spring St.

BEAUTY PARLORS
Louise—902 Innesfallen Ave.

BARBER SHOPS
Payden's—So. Center St.

GARAGES
Green's—1100 S. Yellow Spring St.

SERVICE STATIONS
Underwood—1303 S. Yellow Spring

STEUBENVILLE

TOURIST HOMES
W. Jackson—648 Adam St.
Mrs. L. Martin—508 Ross St.
D. H. Madison—953 Sherman Ave.
H. Jackson—650 Adam St.

TOLEDO

HOTELS
Pleasant, 15 N. Erie St.

TOURIST HOMES
Mrs. E. D. Jackson—
911 City Park Ave.
Mrs. B. F. McWilliams—
639 Indiana Ave.
G. Davis— 532 Woodland Ave.

ZANESVILLE

HOTELS
Park, 1561 W. Main St.
Stevens, 657 W. Main St.

TOURIST HOMES
Mrs. A. M. Thomas—
12 Sharon Ave.
Mrs. L. E. Coston—
641 W. Main St.

WARREN

RESTAURANTS
Lynum & Germans'
Cocktail Baar—644 Pine Ave. S. E.

OKLAHOMA

ENID

TOURIST HOMES
McFall's Apartments
202 E. Park St.
Allen Crumb—222 E. Park St.
Mrs. Eliza Baty—520 E. State St.
Mrs. Ware—712 E. Park St.

Mrs. Ed. Johnson—
210 E. Market St.
Mrs. Elsie Gabble—502 E. Wabash
Edwards—222 E. Park St.

ROAD HOUSES
Cabbell—5th & Ohio Sts.

NIGHTS CLUBS
Cabbells—S. 4th St.

BARBER SHOPS
Baker—418 E. Wabash

SERVICE STATIONS
Vandorf—Broadway & Washington

GUTHRIE

TOURIST HOMES
Mrs. Celia James—
1002 E. Springer Ave.
Mrs. M. A. Smith—317 S. 2nd St.
Mrs. Martha Jordan—304 S. 2nd St.

MUSKOGEE

HOTELS
Elliot's—111½ S. 2nd St.
Bozeman
Peoples—316 N. 2nd St.

TAVERN
Crazy Rock Inn—318 N. 2nd St.

OKLAHOMA CITY

HOTELS
Hall—308½ N. Central
Littlepage—219 N. Central St.
New Acacia—323 E. 2nd St.
Parker—1st & Stiles
M. and M 219 N. Central
Bethel Rooms—326½ E. 2nd St.
Magnolia Inn—629 E. 4th
William Rooms—323 E. 2nd St.

TAVERN
Lyons Cafe—304 E. 2nd St.

BEAUTY PARLORS
Chambers—531 N. Kelly St.

AUTOMOTIVES
Deep Rock Oil Corp.—40 E. 2nd St.

OKMULGEE

HOTELS
Creek—620 E. 4th St.

SHAWNEE

HOTELS
Ollison—501 S. Bell St.

TOURIST HOMES
M. Gross—602 S. Bell St.

TULSA

HOTELS
Small—615 E. Archer St.
Lincoln—E. Archer St.
Red Wing—206 N. Greenwood
Royal—605 E. Asher St.
Manard—922 E. Mashill Fl.
McHunt—1121 N. Grenwood Ave.

TOURIST HOMES
Mrs. W. H. Smith—
124½ N. Greenwood
Mrs. Thomas Gentry—
537 N. Detroit Ave.
Mrs. C. L. Netherland—
542 N. Elgin St.

RESTAURANTS
Your Cab—517 E. Beady St.
Barbeque—
1111 N. Greenwood Av.

BEAUTY PARLORS
Mrs. Smiths'—524 E. Jasper
Cotton Bossom—
106 N. Greenwood Ave.
Mrs. J. C. Mays'—
523 N. Greenwood Ave.

BARBER SHOP
Leader—203 N. Greenwood

TAVERNS
Del Rio Bar—
1448 N. Greenwood Ave.

SERVICE STATIONS
Mince—2nd & Elgin Sts.

GARAGES
Pine St.—906 E. Pine St.
L & M—617 E. Cameron St.

DRUG STORES
Meharry Drugs—
101 Greenwood Ave.

WEWOKA

HOTELS
Carter

OREGON

PORTLAND

HOTELS
Golden West—Broadway & Everett
Medley—2272 N. Interstate Ave.

PENNSYLVANIA

ALLENTOWN

TOURIST HOMES
Mrs. D. Taliaferro, 378 Union St.

BEDFORD

HOTELS
Harris—200 West St.

BRISTOL

TOURIST HOMES
Mrs. L. Willhite, 414 Cedar St.

COATESVILLE

HOTELS
Subway

CHAMBERSBURG

HOTELS
Liberty Inn, Liberty & Water St.

TOURIST HOMES
Mrs. H. Pinns, 68 W. Liberty St.
Mrs. C. Stevenson, 619 S. Main St.

CHESTER

RESTAURANTS
Rio—321 Central Ave.
Phillips—1712 W. 3rd St.

TAVERNS
Wright's—
West 3rd St. & Central

BARBER SHOPS
Bouldin—1710 West 3rd St.

BEAUTY PARLOR
Rosella—413 Concord Ave.
Alex. Davis—123 Reaney St.

SERVICE STATIONS
Barnett—7th & Central

TAILORS
Tailor Shop—515 Central Ave.

WEST CHESTER

HOTELS
Magnolia, 300 E. Miner St.

DARBY

TAVERNS
Golden Star—
10th & Forrester Ave.

ERIE

HOTELS
Pope, 1318 French St.

TOURIST HOMES
Mrs. Famble—538 West 12th St.

AUTOMOTIVES
Craig Oil Co.—433 N Main St.

HAMSBURG

HOTELS
Al Duffin—144 Balm St.

GETTYBURG

TOURIST HOMES
Mrs. J. Forsett—210 W. High St.

HARRISBURG

HOTELS
Alexander—7th & Boas Sts.
Jackson, 1004 N. 6th St.

TOURIST HOMES
Mrs. H. Carter, 606 Foster St.
Mrs. H. Hall, Herr & Montgomery
Mrs. W. D. Jones—
613 forster St.

LANCASTER

TOURIST HOMES
Mrs. E. Clark, 462 Rockland St.
J. Carter, 143 S. Duke St.
A. L. Polite, 540 North St.

OIL CITY

TOURIST HOMES
Mrs. Jackson, 258 Bissel Ave.
Mrs. M. Moore, 8 Bishop St.

PHILADELPHIA

HOTELS
Attucks—8015 S. 15th St.
Baltimore, 1438 Lombard St.
Citizens, 420 S. 15th St.
Douglas, Broad & Lombard Sts.
Elrae, 805 N. 13th St,
Elizaeth Fry, 756 S. 16th St.
La Salle, 2026 Ridge Ave.
Maceo Cafe, Van Pelt & Norris St.
New Roadside, 514 S. 15th St.
Paradise, 1627 Fitzwater St.
The Alston, 2333 Catherine St.
Y. M. C. A.,1724 Christian St.
Y. W. C. A.,1605 Catherine St.
Y. W. C. A., 6128 Germantown Ave.
Horseshoe—12th & Lombard
New Phain—2059 Fitzwater St.
La Reve—Cor. 9 & Columbus Ave.
Dupree—Broad & South Sts.

TAVERNS
Cotton Grove—1329 South St.
Loyal Grill—16th & South Sts.
Lyons Cafe—1418 South St.
National Cafe—1th & Fitzwater
Wayside Inn—13th & Oxford Sts.
Dixon's Wonder Bar,
19th & Montgomery Sts.
Lenox, Popular — Jessup Sts.
Roseland, 5404 Arch St.
Sam's, 1612 South St.
Wander Inn, 18th & Federal Sts.

NIGHT CLUBS
Butler's Paradise, Ridge &
Jefferson
The Progressive Club,
1415 S. 20th St.

RESTAURANTS
Marion's, 20th & Bainridge Sts.
Wilson's, 21st & Burke Sts.

BARBER SHOPS
S. Jones, 2064 Ridge St.

BEAUTY PARLORS
Agnes—1811 Bainbridge St.
At's, 661 N. 13th St.

Effie's, 5502 Girad Ave.
Elizabeth's, 5003 Brown St.
A. Henson, 1318 Fairmont Ave.
Jennie's, 1618 French St.
La Salle, 2036 Ridge St.
Lady Ross, 718 S. 18th St.
Reynolds—1612 N. 13th St.
Redmond's, 710 N. 48th St.
Rose's, 16th & South Sts.
F. Franklin—2115 W. York St.
A. B. Tooks—916 S. 17th St.
R. Morton's—
17th & Bainbridge Sts.

AUTOMOTIVES
United Oil—16th & Fitzwater

GARAGES
Booker Bros—1811 Fitzwater St.
Garage—5732 Westminister Ave.
Garage—1823 Bainbridge St.

SERVICE STATIONS
Dorsey Bros., 2009 Oxford St.

GERMANTOWN PHIL

TOURIST HOMES
M. Foote—5560 Blakmore St.

BARBER SHOPS
G. Taylor, 60 W. Duval St.

BEAUTY PARLORS
M. Harris—260 Arnot St.

TAVERNS
The Terrace Grill,
75 E. Sharpnack St.

PITTSBURGH

HOTELS
Ave—1538 Wylie Ave.
Bailey's Stagg, 1308 Wylie Ave.
Bailey's, 1533 Center Ave.
Colonial, Wylie Ave. & Fulton St.
Park, 2215 Wylie Ave.
Potter, 1304 Wylie Ave.
Station—Station St. East End

TOURIST HOMES
Mrs. R. Lewis, 2600 Wylie Ave.
B. William—68 Fullerton St.
Mrs. William—5518 Claybourne St.

RESTAURANTS
Dearing's—2524 Wylie Ave.

BEAUTY PARLORS
Orchid—1709 Wylie Ave.
Charlotte's—2639 Wylie Ave.

GARAGES
Wylie's—Wylie Ave.—
Bet. Wash & Fernands.

SERVICE STATIONS
Scotty's—2414 Centre Ave.

READING

TOURIST HOMES
C. Dawson, 441 Buttonwood St.

SCRANTON

TOURIST HOMES

MRS. ELVIRA KING
1312 LINDEN STREET

Mrs. Jenkins—610 N. Wash Ave.
Mrs. J. Taylor—1415 Penn Ave.

SHARON HILL

TAVERNS
Dixie Cafe—
Hook Rd. — Howard St.

WASHINGTON

HOTELS
Jimmie Fishers, 120 E. Chestnut St

TOURIST HOMES

MRS. ANNA V. BANKS
140 E. CHESTNUT ST.

B. T. Washington—32 N. College

RESTAURANTS
W. Allen, N. Lincoln St.
J. Fisher, 120 E. Chestnut St.
M. Thomas, N. Lincoln St.
Lincoln—N. Elm St.

NIGHT CLUBS
Dreamland Inn, E. Hallan Ave.

BARBER SHOPS
Yancey's, E. Spruce St.
T. Wheeler, E. Chestnut St.
J. Baker, E. Chestnut St.

WILLIAMSPORT

TOURIST HOMES
Mrs. W. Gordon—646 Walnut St.
M. Nash, 612 Walnut St.
Mrs. E. Johnson, 621 Spruce St.

WILKES BARRE

HOTELS
Shaw, 15 S. State St.

YORK

HOTELS
Howard, Beaver & Princess Sts.
Y. W. C. A., N. Lincoln St.

TOURIST HOMES
Mrs. E. Armstrong, 116 E. King St.
Mrs. I. Grayson, 32 W. Princess
John Miller, 307 E. King St.

"EXPERIENCES"

"The Green Book" will pay $5.00 for manuscripts accepted by the publishers. Subjects based on Negro motoring conditions, scenic wonders in your travels, places visited of interest and one's motoring experiences.

RHODE ISLAND

NEWPORT

HOTELS
Glover, Brindley & Center Sts.

TOURIST HOMES
Mrs. F. Jackson—28 Hall Ave.
Mrs. R. Craddle—165 Spring St.
Mrs. C. F. Burton—7 De Blois St
Mrs. L. Jackson—35 Bath Road

PROVIDENCE

HOTELS
Hill Top Inn, 72 Meeting St.
The Bertha, 54 Meeting St.

TOURIST HOMES
Mrs. M. A. Greene—58 Meeting St.
W. W. Joyce—24 Camp St.
Dinah's—462—4 N. Main

RESTAURANTS
Dickerson's—28½ Cranston St.

BEAUTY PARLORS
B. Boyd's—43 Camp St.
Geraldine's—205 Thurbus Ave.
Lucille's—477 N. Main St.

AUTOMOBILES
George's—203 Plainfield St.

SOUTH CAROLINA

AIKEN

TOURIST HOMES
Mrs. C. F. Holland—1118 Richland Ave.
Mrs. M. H. Harrison, Richland Avenue

ROAD HOUSES
Chauffeurs Inn, 1102 Sumter Street

SERVICE STATIONS
Mitchell's—V. S. I. York St.

DRUG STORES
Dr. C. C. Johnson's—Richland Ave.

BEAUFORD

TOURIST HOMES
D. Brown's

SERVICE STATIONS
Peoples—D. Brown. Prop.

CHARLESTON

TOURIST HOMES
Mrs. Alston, 43 South St.
Mrs. Gladsden, 15 Nassau St.
Mrs. H. L. Harleston, 250 Ashley Avenue
Mrs. Mayes, 47 Sotuh Street.

TAVERNS
Green Grill—186 Spring St.
Harleston's Villa—250 Ashley Ave.

TAXICABS
First Class—242 Ashley St.

COLUMBIA

HOTELS
TAYLOR, 1016 Washington St.

TOURIST HOMES
Mrs. H. Cornwell, 1713 Wayne
Mrs. W. D. Chappelle, 1301 Pine St.
Mrs. B. Vincent, 1712 Wayne
Mrs. J. P. Wakefield, 1323 Heidt St.
Mrs. S. H. Smith—929 Pine St.

RESTAURANTS
Green Leaf—1117 Washington St.

TAVERNS
College Inn—1609 Hardin St.

SERVICE STATIONS
Waverley—2200 Taylor St.
A. W. Simpkin's—1331 Park St.

BARBER SHOPS
Holman's—2103 Gervias St.

BEAUTY PARLORS
Ruth's—1221 Pine St.
Mme. Peters—1906 Blanding St.

TAXICABS
Black Diamond—Washington St.
Blue Ribbon—1072 Washington St.

DRUG STORES
Thomas' Drug Store
Counts'—1105 Washington St.

FLORENCE

TOURIST HOMES
Mrs. C. C. Godblood, 227 E. Marion
Mrs. B. Wright, 1004 E. Cheeve St.

GEORGETOWN

TOURIST HOMES
Mrs. R. Anderson, 424 Broad
Mrs. D. Atkinson, 811 Duke
Jas. Becote, 118 Oronge
T. W. Brown, Merriman & Emanuel
Mrs. A. A. Smith, 317 Emanuel

GREENVILLE

HOTELS
Imperial—8 Nelson St.
Poinsette—11 S. Hudson St.

MULLENS

HOTELS
283 W. Front St.

SPARTANBURG

TOURIST HOMES
- Mrs. L. Johnson—307 W. Dean St.
- Mrs. O. Jones—255 N. Dean St.
- Mrs. S. McElroy, Silver Hill St.
- Mrs. M. Young, S. Liberty St.
- Mrs. M. H. Wright, 490 S. Liberty St.

RESTAURANTS
- Beatty—N. View

SERVICE STATIONS
- Collins—398 S. Liberty
- Service & Cab—114 Short Wafford St.

GARAGES
- Jones—255 N. Dean St.

BEAUTY PARLORS
- Harmon—221 N. Dean St.

SUMTER

TOURIST HOMES
- Mrs. C. H. Bracey—210 W. Oakland Ave.
- Mrs. J. Boyd—504 Main St.

SOUTH DAKOTA

SIOUX FALLS

TOURIST HOMES
- Service Center—415 So. 1st Ave.
- Mrs. J. Moxley—915 N. Main

TENNESSEE

CHATTANOOGA

HOTELS
- Lincoln, 1101 Carter St.
- Martin, 204 E. 9th St.
- Peoples, 1104 Carter St.

TOURIST HOMES
- Mrs. J. Baker, 843 E. 8th St.
- Mrs. E. Brown, 1133 E. 8th St.
- Mrs. D. Lowe, 803 Fairview Ave.
- Y. W. C. A., 839 E. 8th St.

TAXICABS
- Simms—915 University St.

BARBER SHOPS
- Wright's—219 E. 9th St.

CLARKSVILLE

HOTELS
- Central, 535 Franklin St.

TOURIST HOMES
- E. F. Thompkins, 411 Poston St
- Mrs. H. Northington, 717 Main St.

BRISTOL

TOURIST HOMES
- A. D. Henderson, 301 McDowell St.

JACKSON

TAXICABS
- Knox Cab Co.—614 Lane Ave.

KNOXVILLE

HOTELS
- Brownlow—219 E. Vine St.

LEXINGTON

TOURIST HOMES
- C. Timberlake, Holly St.

MEMPHIS

HOTELS
- Clarke, 144 Beale Ave.
- Travelers—347 Vance

RESTAURANTS
- The Parkview—516 N. 3rd St.

TAILORS
- Parks—697 Laumderdale

DRUG STORES
- So. Memphis—907 Florida Ave.

MURFREESBORO

TOURIST HOMES
- Mrs. R. Moore, Cor. University & State Sts.
- Mrs. F. Hoover—439 E. State St.

NASHVILLE

HOTELS
- Bryant, 500 8th Ave. S.
- Fred Douglas, 501 4th Ave.
- Grace—1122 Cedar St.

TOURIST HOMES
- Mrs. E. Wood—1408 [illegible] llps St.

BEAUTY PARLORS
- Queen of Shebra—500—8th Ave. So.
- Estelle—419—4th Ave. Rm. 305

TEXAS

ABILENE

TAVERNS
- Hammond Cafe—620 Plum St.

AUSTIN

TOURIST HOMES
- Mrs. R. S. Lovingood—803 E. 13th
- Mrs. J. W. Frazier—810 E. 13th
- Mrs. J. W. Duncan—1214 E. 7th
- Mrs. W. M. Tears—1203 E. 12th

BEAUMONT

RESTAURANTS
- Long Bar—b—q—539 Forsythe St.

CORSICANA

TOURISTS HOMES
Rev. Conner—E. 4th Ave.
S. J. Chestnut—616 E. 5th Ave.
Robt. Lee—712 E. 4th

DALLAS

HOTELS
Grand Terrace—Boll & Juliett
Lewis—302½ North Central St.
Powell—3115 State St.
Palm Hotel
Hall's—1801 Hall St.

RESTAURANTS
Beaumont Barbeque
1815 Orange St.
Tommie & Fred's—
Wash St. & Thomas Ave.
Irene's—3209 Thomas Ave.
Davis—6806 Lemmon Ave.
Palm Cafe—2213 Halls St.

TAVERNS
Hall St.—1804 Hall St.

BEAUTY PARLORS
S. Brown's—1721 Hall St.

BARBER SHOPS
Washington's—3203 Thomas Ave.

NIGHT CLUBS
Regal—Thomas Ave. & Hall St

DRUG STORES
Smith's—Cor. Hall St. & Thomas Ave.

SERVICE STATIONS
Walton's—2400 Thomas Ave.
Walker's—2307 Hall St.
William's—Cor. Lennard & Thomas Ave.
Jack's—Hall & Central Ave.

GARAGES
Givens—3102 Ross Ave.

TAXICABS
State—2411 Elm St.

EL PASO

HOTELS
Daniel—413 S. Oregon St.
Murrays—218½ Mesa St.
Scott—218 S. Mesa Ave.
Jordan's—104 Kemp St.

TOURIST HOMES
Mrs. B. F. Phillips—
704 S. St. Vrain St.
Mrs. C. Williams—
1507 Wyoming St.
Mrs. L. Walker—
2923 E. San Antonio
Mrs. S. W. Stull—
511 Tornillo

TAVERNS
Daniel's—403 S. Orange St

TAILORS
Handy Dandy—307 S. Orange St.

DRUG STORES
Donnel—3301 Nanzana St.

FORT WORTH

HOTELS
Del Rey—901 Jones St.
Jim—413-15 E. Fifth St.

TOURIST HOMES
Evan's—1213 E. Terrell St.

SERVICE STATIONS
South Side—970 E. Humboldt St.

GALVESTON

HOTELS
Oleander—421½—25th St.

TOURIST HOMES
Miss G. H. Freeman—
1414—29th St.
Mrs. J. Pope—2824 Ave. M.

TAVERNS
Gulf View
28th & Boulevard Houston

HOUSTON

HOTELS
Coopers—1011 Dart St.
Dowling—3111 Dowling St.
The Oriental—421 San Felipe St.

BEAUTY PARLORS
School & Parlor—502 Louisiana St.
Alma's—2736 Lyons Yes

RESTAURANTS
Cottage Inn—2219 Gray Ave.

TAVERNS
Welsome Cafe—2409 Pease Ave.
Allen's—2402 Elgin Yes
Ballard"s—1805 Gregg Yes

DRUG STORES
Langford's—2409 Pease Ave.

MARSHALL

TOURIST HOMES
Rev. Bailey—1103 W. Grand Ave.

HELPFUL?

Use it on Your Next Trip

Use It When You are Out for a ride

MEXIA

HOTELS
Carlton—201 W. Commerce St.

TOURIST HOMES
C. Shannon—112 S. Belknap St.
S. P. Miller—302 N. Denton St.
L. Ransom—119 N. Denton St.

MIDLAND

HOTELS
Watson's Hotel

BEAUTY PARLORS
Beauty Shop Jeanetta

PARIS

HOTELS
Brownrigg—88 N. 22nd St.
Dixon—22nd & Booth Sts.

TOURIST HOMES
Mrs. I. Scott—115 N. 22nd St.

PITTSBURG

TOURIST HOMES
Mrs. S. E. Crawford—Happy Hollow

SAN ANTONIO

TOURIST HOMES
Miss L. Brown—1216 Dawson St.
Mrs. M. Lawson—245 Canton St.
R. Banks—127 N. Mesquite St.

TYLER

TOURIST HOMES
Mrs. Thomas—516 N. Border St.
Mrs. W. Langston—1010 N. Border St.

TEXARKANA

HOTELS
Brown—312½ Elm St.

WACO

TOURIST HOMES
B. Ashford—902 N. 8th St.

RESTAURANT
Ideal—107 N. 2nd St.

BEAUTY PARLORS
Cendivilla—107½ N. 2nd St.

BARBER SHOPS
Satchell's—329 S. 2nd St.

GARAGES
Edward's—1029 Elm St.

WAXAHACHIE

TOURIST HOMES
Mrs. A. Nunn—413 E. Main St.
Mrs. M. Johnson—427 E. Main St.
Mrs. N. Lowe—418 E. Main St.
Mrs. N. Jones—430 E. Main St.

WICHITA FALLS

TOURIST HOMES
E. B. Jeffrey—509 Juarez St.
T. S. Jackson—303 Park St.

AMARILLO

HOTELS
Watley's—112 Van Buren St.

RESTAURANTS
Harlem Grill—114 Harrison St.

UTAH

SALT LAKE CITY

VERMONT

BURLINGTON

HOTELS
The Pates—86-90 Archibald St.

RUTLAND

TOURIST HOMES
J. H. Meade—83 Strongs Ave.

RESTAURANTS
White House—50 W. Washington St.

VIRGINIA

ABINGDON

TOURIST HOMES
Mrs. H. Anderson, Near Fairgrounds, E. End.
Mrs. N. Brown, High St.
Mrs. A. Monroe, 300 "A" St.
B. Nicholas, Park St.

ALEXANDRIA

TOURIST HOMES
J. T. Holms, 803 Gibbon St.
J. A. Barrett, 724 Gibbon St.

BRISTOL

HOTELS
Palace, 210 Front St.

CARET

TAVERNS
Sessons Tavern

CHARLOTTESVILLE

TOURIST HOMES
Workman—129 Preston Ave.
Virinia Inn—W. Main St.
Alexander's—413 Dyce St.

BARBER SHOPS
Jokers—North 4th St.

BEAUTY PARLORS
Apex—211 W. Main St.

CHRISTIANBURG

HOTELS
Eureka

DANVILLE

TOURIST HOMES
Mrs. Yancey—320 Holbrook St.
Mrs. P. M. Logan—
328 N. Union St.
Mrs. M. K. Page, 434 Holbrook St.
Mrs. S. A. Overbey, Holbrook St.

DUNBARTON

TOURIST HOMES
H. Jackson—Rt. No. 1 Box 322

FARMVILLE

TAVERNS
Ried's—200 Block, Main St.

SERVICE STATIONS
Clark's—Main St.

FREDERICKSBURG

HOTELS
McGuire, 521 Princess Ann St.
Rappshsnock, 520 Princess Ann St.

TOURIST HOMES
Mrs. B. Scott, 207 5th St.

HARRISONBURG

TOURIST HOMES
Mrs. Johnson—371 N. Federal St.

RESTAURANTS
Frank's—145 E. Wolf St.

LEXINGTON

TOURIST HOMES
The Franklin—9 Tucker St.

TAVERNS
Rose Inn—331 N. Main St.

LYNCHBURG

HOTELS
Manhattan, 1001 5th St.
Petersburg—66 9th St.

TOURIST HOMES
Mrs. C. Harper, 1109 8th St.
Mrs. M. Thomas, 919 Polk
Mrs. Smith, 504 Jackson
Happyland Lake Home—812 5th Ave.

ROAD HOUSES
Goldendale Inn, 1001 5th St.

TAVERNS
King's—5th & Monroe

BEAUTY PARLORS
Selma's, 1002 5th St.

SERVICE STATIONS
United—1016 Fifth St.

NATURAL BRIDGE

TOURIST HOMES
Mountain View Cottage

NEWPORT NEWS

TOURIST HOMES
Mrs. W. E. Barron, 758 25th St.
Mrs. W. R. Cooks, 2211 Marshall A.
Mrs. W. Herndon, 753 26th St.
Mrs. C. Stephents, 1909 Marshall A.
Mrs. J. H. Taliaferro,
2206 Marshall Ave.

RESTAURANTS
Tavern Rest—2108 Jefferson

TAVERNS
Rosetta Inn—2116 Marshall Ave.
Ritz—636 25th St.

BEAUTY PARLORS
Rattrie's, 300 Chestnut Ave.

SERVICE STATIONS
Ridley's, Orcutt Ave. & 30th St.

NORFOLK

HOTELS
Douglas, 716 Smith St.
Wheatley—Brambleton Ave.
Tatum's Inn—453 Brewer St.
Prince George, 1751 Church St.
Huntersville—Church St.

TOURIST HOMES
Mrs. S. Noble—723 Chaple St.

RESTAURANTS
Sunlight—1053 Church St.

BEAUTY PARLORS
Jordan's—526 Brambleton Ave.
Vel-Ber St. Ann—1008 Church St.
Yeargen's—1685 Church St.

TAVERNS
Peoples, Church & Calvert Sts.
Russell's—835 Church St.

SERVICE STATIONS

ALSTON'S ESSO SERVICE
CHURCH ST., Cor. 20th St.

SERVICE STATIONS
Mac's—1625 Church St.

PETERSBURG

HOTELS
The Walker House, 116 South
TOURIST HOMES
Mrs. E. Johnson, 116 South Ave.
NIGHT CLUBS
Chatter Boy—143 Harrison St.

PHOEBUS

RESTAURANTS
Ye Shingle Inn, 17 E. County St.

RICHMOND

HOTELS
Miller's & Archers—3rd & Clay
Slaughters, 514 N. 2nd St.
TOURIST HOMES
Mrs. E. Brice, 14 W. Clay St.
Y. W. C. A., 515 N. 7th St.
RESTAURANTS
Cora's Waffle Shop, Leigh & 5th St
BEAUTY PARLORS
Rest- A- Bit, 619 N. 3rd St.
SERVICE STATIONS
Preston St.—2nd & Preston Sts.
Cameron's—Brook Ave. & W. Clay St.
Harris—400 N. Henry St.
BARBER SHOPS
Wright's—412 E. Leigh St.

ASHLAND

SOUTH HILL

HOTELS
Brown's—Melvin Brown, Prop.
Groom's—John Groom, Prop.

NIGHT CLUBS
Spot Tavern—Rt. No. 58—E. of So. Hill.

ROANOKE

HOTELS
Dumas—Henry St. N.W.
TOURIST HOMES
Reynolds—34 Well Ave. N. W.
TAVERNS
Tom's Place
GARAGES
Maple Leaf—High St. at Henry

STAUNTON

HOTELS
Pannell's Inn, 613 N. Augusta St.
RESTAURANTS
Johnson's—301 N. Central Ave.

TAPPAHANNOCK

HOTELS
McGuire's Inn—Marsh St.

WINCHESTER

HOTELS
New Evans Hotel, Sharp St.
TOURIST HOMES
Mrs. Jos. Willis, N. Main St.
Dunbar Tea Room, 21 W. Hart St.
RESTAURANTS
Ruth's—128 E. Cecil St.

WASHINGTON

EVERETT

TOURIST HOMES
Mrs. J. Samuels—2214 Wedmore Ave.
Mrs. J. T. Payne—2132 Oaks Ave.
Mrs. G. Samuels—3620 Hoyt Ave.

SEATTLE

HOTELS
Golden West—416 Seventh Ave. So.
Coast—901 King St.

TACOMA

TOURIST HOMES
Mrs. A. Robinson—1906 S. "I" St.
Mrs. J. H. Carter—1017 S. Trafton St.

WALLA WALLA

TOURIST HOMES
Wayside Inn—1107 W. Willow

YAKIMA

TOURIST HOMES
H. C. Deering—508 S. 3rd St.
L. A. Branum—515 S. 1st
Mrs. T. Jones—906 Naches Ave.
Mrs. W. H. Jones—310 Third Ave.

WEST VIRGINIA

BECKLEY

HOTELS
New Pioneer—58 S. Fayette St.
RESTAURANTS
Home Service—37 Prince St.
SERVICE STATIONS
Moss's—135 S Fayette St.

BLUEFIELD

TOURIST HOMES
Traveler's Inn—602 Raleigh St.

CHARLESTON

HOTELS
Ferguson
TOURIST HOMES
A. Brown, 1001 Washington St.
TAVERNS
White Front—1007 Washington St.
Palace Cafe—910 Washington St.

FAIRMONT

HOTELS
Cobbs—226 Jackson St.

HUNTINGTON

HOTELS
Southern—921 8th Ave.
Fair
Massey's, 837 7th Ave.
The Ross, 911 8th Ave.
TOURIST HOMES
E. Washington, 1657 8th Ave.
Mrs. R. J. Lewis—1412 10th Ave.
Mrs. C. J. Barnett—810 7th Ave.
Mrs. Jones—1824 10th ave.
Mrs. B. Bowling—1517 8th Ave.
RESTAURANTS
J. Gross, 839 7th Ave.
TAVERNS
Monroe's, 1616 8th Ave.
The Alpha—1624 8th Ave.
NIGHT CLUBS
Appomattox Club, 1659 8th Ave.
BARBER SHOPS
J. Harriston, 1615 8th Ave.
BEAUTY PARLORS
Mrs. Pack, 1612 Artisen Ave.
SERVICE STATION
Sterling, Cor 12th St. & 3rd Ave.
GARAGE
South Side, 716 8th Ave.

HARPERS FERRY

HOTELS
River View Lodge—Storer Colege
Hilltop House—Mrs. Drew

WELCH

HOTELS
Capheart—14 Virginia Ave.

WHEELING

HOTELS
Verse—1042 Market
TOURIST HOMES
Mrs. W. Turner—114 12th St.
Mrs. C. Early—132 12th St.
Mrs. R. Williams—
1007 Chapline St.
Mrs. J. T. Hughes—1021 Goff St.
RESTAURANTS
Singetlery—1043 Chapline St.
NIGHT CLUBS
American Legion—1516 Main St.
Elks Club—1010 Chapline St.
BEAUTY PARLORS
Miss Hall—Chapline St.
Miss Taylor—Chapline St.

WISCONSIN

FOND DU LAC

TOURIST HOMES
Mrs. E. Pirtle—45 E. 11th St.
Mrs. V. Williams—
97 S. Seymour St.

OSHKOSH

TOURIST HOMES
L. Shadd—37 King St.
F. Pemberton—239 Liberty St.

WYOMING

CASPER

TOURIST HOMES
Mrs. J. E. Edwards—347 N. Grant
H. Keeling—331 N. Grant

CHEYENNE

HOTELS
Barbeque Inn—622 W. 20th St.
TOURIST HOMES
Mrs. I. Randall—612 W. 18th St.
Mrs. M. Herman—621 W. 18th St.

ROCK SPRINGS

TOURIST HOMES
Mrs. R. Collins—905 6th St.

HISTORY

The Negro Motorist Green Book, first published in 1936, was a product of the rising African-American middle class having the finances and vehicle for travel but facing a world where social and legal resirictions barred them from many accomodations. At the time, there were thousands of "sundown towns", towns where African Americans were legally barred from spending the night there at all.

Victor H. Green
1892 – 1960

The book provided a guide to hotels and restaurant that would accept their business, often ones established specifically for the black customer. Published annually by Victor Hugo Green, a New Yorker who retired from his work as a mailman based on its success and expanded into the travel reservation business, the *Green Book* was for decades a vital handbook, fading out of business only after the civil rights laws of the 1960s brought about the end of legal segregation. It was sold largely through mail order and through service stations - specifically, through Esso stations, as Esso not only served African-American customers, they were willing to franchise their stations to African-Americans, unlike most petroleum companies of the day. The guide was also offered by AAA and distributed elsewhere with advice from the United States Travel Bureau, a government agency

Recommended Readings

- The Teachings of Ptahhotep: The Oldest Book in the World

- The Five Negro Presidents: According to what White People Said They Were

- 100 Amazing Facts About the Negro with Complete Proof: A Short Cut to The World History of The Negro

- From Babylon to Timbuktu: A History of the Ancient Black Races Including the Black Hebrews

CPSIA information can be obtained
at www.ICGtesting.com
Printed in the USA
LVHW091258270219
608919LV00004B/9/P

9 781684 116560